Music of Another World

Szymon
Music of

Translated by

Northwestern University

Laks
Another World

Chester A. Kisiel

Press   Evanston, Illinois

Northwestern University Press
Evanston, Illinois 60201

Originally published as *Musiques d'un autre monde*, Mercure de France, Paris, 1948. Translation © 1989 by Northwestern University Press. All rights reserved.

Printed in the United States of America

Library of Congress Cataloging-in-Publication Data

Laks, Szymon, 1901–
  [Musiques d'un autre monde. English]
  Music of another world / Szymon Laks ; translated by Chester A. Kisiel.
    p.   cm.
  Translation of: Musiques d'un autre monde.
  ISBN 0-8101-0841-0.—ISBN 0-8101-0842-9 (pbk.)
  1. Laks, Szymon, 1901–   . 2. Auschwitz (Poland : Concentration camp) 3. Holocaust, Jewish (1939–1945)—Personal narratives. 4. Composers—Poland—Biography. 5. Music—Poland—Oświęcim—History—20th century. I. Title.
D805.P7L34313 1989
940.53'18—dc20   89-16186
                                                                      CIP

To my friends, comrades in misery

Tadeusz Jawor

Jan Stojakowski

Ludwik Żuk-Skarszewski

I dedicate this selection of memories

Contents

Overture

◆   ◆   ◆

SHORTLY AFTER MY RETURN FROM THE CONCENTRATION CAMP Auschwitz II–Birkenau, I, together with my camp companion René Coudy, wrote a small book, in French, about the orchestra that had existed in the camp and about the kinds of music that had been played there. It was published in 1948 by the Paris publisher Mercure de France as *Musiques d'un autre monde*. It has been out of print for a long time, but there are probably some copies scattered about the world and on library shelves. I have only one copy left.

In the 1950s I began corresponding with people in Poland about the eventual publication of a Polish translation of the book. They answered that the copy I sent had been passed on to the Ministry of Culture and Art, the only body empowered to express an opinion on the usefulness of this kind of publication.

Much time passed—a year? two?—before I finally received the decision of the ministry. I had expected a different kind of refusal, but the opinion expressed by competent circles of the ministry surprised and saddened me very much. The answer was (I quote from memory, for I did not keep the letter), "A too-idyllic book. The Germans are presented in an overly favorable light, and the prisoners as creatures devoid of all feelings of morality and human dignity. Unfit for publication."

At first I did not understand what these gentlemen had in mind, but I soon found the key: the book supposedly suggested to the reader that the Germans—our executioners—hungered for music, while their victims thought about nothing else but filling their stomachs. Shocking! Things could not be put in this way. It would be tantamount to idealizing the hangmen and degrading the already degraded martyrs.

I renewed my efforts in 1967–68. These were not good years. There was an exchange of letters for many months with Poland. Once I was even called on by a Polish woman (visiting Paris on other business) who discussed with me a number of details concerning publication. Not only did I find out nothing new, but for the first time I had a face-to-face encounter with a classic example of "hot air," about which I had heard and read so much. Phrases, generalities, the runaround, sermonizing, all wrapped in an impenetrable fog. Only one thing was clear to me: the book had no chance of appearing in Polish—in Poland.

There was nothing else for me to do but give up the project, and I stopped thinking about it.

✦ ✦ ✦

During the decades that separate us from the "concentration camp era," numerous books, studies, brochures, and articles have appeared about the camps; and quite a few stage plays, movies, and television shows have been produced. All of them talk about the same things, the same facts, but each one of them differently somehow, as though these things and facts were not the same. Between one account and another there are often glaring contradictions that, as far as I know, have not been resolved. Why is this?

As regards the history of the camps, my explanation is that

the author-chroniclers, with greater or lesser talent but for the most part with the same pathos, described events about which they said at the same time, especially if they were eyewitnesses, that "this cannot be described, for there are no words for it." And in fact, how can one describe things that "cannot be described" and for which "there are no words"?

But words must be found, for besides words there is almost nothing—at most a few genuine documentary films and also quite a few "feature" films, hence not genuine, which were supposed to re-create the "gone with the wind" reality. And so every author used words that "did not exist" but that were within his scale of possibilities and within his knowledge of the facts. Thus contradictions were unavoidable.

The book I present to readers interested in these matters does not claim to solve them. On the contrary, it may even introduce a few new contradictions. Is not one of them the very fact that music—that most sublime expression of the human spirit—also became entangled in the hellish enterprise of the extermination of millions of people and even took an active part in this extermination? Most of the books on the German concentration camps mention in passing, as it were, that in some of them there existed larger or smaller musical groups whose role was to play marches to accompany the departure for and return from work of individual units or "commands." There are many publications that claim, not without a certain emphasis, that music kept up the spirits of the emaciated prisoners and gave them the strength to survive. Others assert that music had a directly opposite effect, that it demoralized the poor wretches and contributed instead to their earlier demise. I personally share the latter opinion. I shall return to this side of the problem later.

As far as I know, there is no book discussing in detail the

real role of music in the life of the camps. Since for a long time I was a member of the orchestra in Auschwitz II and during a certain period its conductor, I regard it as my obligation to relate and in some way to commemorate this strange chapter in the history of music, a chapter that will probably not be written by any professional historian of this branch of art.

Nearly forty years have passed since the events I intend to describe. During that time many things have changed in this godly and human world, a little for the better, much for the worse. Horizons have changed, and reflections on what happened then and is still happening today have not ceased for an instant. Hence this book is not an ordinary English version of the French original. The facts are more or less the same, but they have been enriched with still other disclosures, documents, and testimonies that have been sent to me over the years.

There are still other reasons that this book, though the Germans and the prisoners are presented in the same way as before, differs from the original: we were all then too close to the physical and moral experiences suffered, we were still in a state of psychological stupor and alienated from our regained freedom. It was difficult for us to evaluate things and people, both those we had left behind and those to which we had returned. Today this stupor, though it will never disappear completely, has considerably abated, and it is easier to look at the events and experiences of those years with a greater dose of objectivity. I say "with a greater dose" since I believe that absolute objectivity will never be possible.

Fate decreed that I had to take up this work alone and decide for myself what to leave in, what to take out, and what to change from the perspective of the past decades. Despite a considerable evolution in my look at certain aspects of camp life, the facts described in the following pages have lost none of their ghastly authenticity. The grotesque clash of music with these facts brings this authenticity into even greater relief. I shall try to spare the reader descriptions of the atrocities of which Auschwitz-Birkenau—like other camps—was the scene. So much has been written about this that it would be hard to add anything new. Besides, a little more, a little less, what's the difference? However, in spite of my sincerest intentions, I shall not be able to omit entirely those "scenic and idyllic pictures": to write about music in Birkenau without referring to the background against which this music was played would be counter to the aim and even the sense of this book.

For this is not a book about *music.* It is a book about *music in a Nazi concentration camp.* One could also say: about *music in a distorting mirror.*

Music of
Another World

◆   ◆   ◆

IN FEBRUARY 1974 ALEKSANDER KULISIEWICZ, A FORMER PRISoner at the Sachsenhausen concentration camp, came from Poland to see me in Paris. I did not know him personally, but I had heard a lot about him, namely, that he was very active in collecting songs, tunes, poetry, and camp music in general in all of its aspects. He had also heard about me, so he expected that I would be able to add to his collection, especially of songs, in which he was most interested. I knew that after the war he had given a few recitals of camp songs in several countries, that he had made a few recordings that were very popular, and that he had devoted all of his efforts after the war to the history of the songs of the resistance movement in the concentration camps.

Unfortunately, I could be of no help to him, first, since in Birkenau I had not encountered any poetic or vocal activity, second, since I had left behind my pile of music paper, written almost entirely in my own hand, when the camp authorities moved us from Birkenau in October 1944. I have no idea what happened to this music, and I never looked into the matter. Perhaps it is in the Auschwitz museum?

This did not prevent Kulisiewicz and me from chatting away about our personal histories from the moment of arrest and deportation to liberation and return home. We also did not fail to touch on "companions of the executioner's trade" each of us had encountered.

At a certain moment Kulisiewicz mentioned a name that set my heart beating faster: Ludwik Żuk-Skarszewski. I asked immediately, almost without thinking, "When did he die?" for during these long years I had before my eyes a picture of Ludwik on a stretcher, being carried to the "Sick Room" (typhus ward), where, I was told, he had died shortly later. "What do you mean, when did he die?" Kulisiewicz asked in surprise. "Well, in what year?" "Ludwik Żuk is still alive, he lives in Chrzanów, he's a schoolteacher in . . ."

I did not hear the rest. Nothing was important but one thing. That Ludwik was alive! Kulisiewicz did not know his address, but he did know that he was a teacher of Polish in the high school in Chrzanów, Kraków Province, and that a letter addressed there would probably reach him.

Does he still remember me? Does he remember how he snatched me, almost dying, from the clutches of a convict detachment and, despite the protests of his superiors, arranged my transfer to the music group of *Notenschreiber*, that is, music copyists? From that time on I no longer went out to physical labor, which saved me from inevitable quick death. After so many years. We had known each other for such a short time, hardly a few months. How could I recall myself to his memory?

I wrote without delay to the address Kulisiewicz had given me. My letter was sent on 10 February 1974; the answer came at the beginning of March. Żuk wrote:

I read your letter with indescribable joy, since like you about me, I had false information about you. Namely, Prof. Lachs, whom I mistakenly took for you, informed my wife that you had perished in Auschwitz. What luck that this turned out to be untrue! After my departure from Birkenau I was in Gross-Rosen, Sachsenhausen, Falkensee, where we worked on the production of tanks and V-2 rockets. There I was also ordered to organize a *Lagerkapelle*, in which there were musicians of worldwide fame as well as Negroes and mulattoes.

I will answer your questions. I was arrested on 15 April 1942 for taking part in underground teaching along with several other professors and after a long interrogation deported to Auschwitz I on 3 June. I was given the number 37,939. There I went through another interrogation about my participation in cultural and social life in Silesia, where I was alleged to have harassed Germans in the secondary school. I somehow emerged from this plight in one piece and after two weeks was sent for punishment to the SK [*Strafkommando*, penal detachment] in Bunawerke [now the Oświęcim Chemical Works]. On 27 June I was badly beaten up by a kapo* for helping a Jew from Paris (whose name I don't remember) and dragged back to the camp along with the corpses of this detachment. I was lying on this heap of bodies when Dr. Wasilewski, who was writing down the numbers of the corpses, stepped on my foot, and it turned out that I was still alive. . . . Since Dr. Wasilewski was in the "VIPs'"** Barracks 24, where Franz Nierychło, kapo of the kitchen and also conductor of the orchestra, lived, I managed to get into the *Lagerkapelle* as a violinist.

Shortly after this, sixteen musicians were selected and sent to Birkenau. Since I was a *Notenschreiber* and arranger, Nierychło chose me to prepare the repertoire, for we had gotten instruments but no music. I had to recall marches and hits from memory, and it was while I was doing this job that you found me in Birkenau.

So for more than thirty years both of us were convinced that the other was not alive. It took Aleksander Kulisiewicz's collecting bug to rekindle a friendship that had been buried so

* A prisoner in charge of a work detachment.
** I.e., for prisoners in higher positions.

long ago. What words should be used to celebrate such rediscoveries? I will not use any.

Since that time we have been writing to each other regularly. I comfort myself to some extent that as the need arises I sent him some medicines and other sundries that are unavailable in Poland and in this way partially pay my debt. But I know that I will never pay it. What is the price of life? One's own life?

Ludwik Żuk is not the only Pole to whom I owe my survival of the Hitlerite pogrom (I will mention others later). As I said, we spent barely a few months together in Birkenau, and the first months at that. After our parting I still faced two and a half years of camp experiences, and during that period I met— as every one of us did—a countless number of human (and inhuman) types of various kinds. Out of this pack several sparkling characters of all different nationalities, including Polish, loom up before me.

It was difficult to preserve even a tiny bit of humanity and love of one's neighbor in this atmosphere of ghastliness and incessant, persistent struggle for a piece of bread, for a sip of water, for life. Every moment was filled with the threat of death. Every minute survived was a gift from heaven. In short, I hardly exaggerate when I say that to survive Auschwitz or the other concentration camps was nothing but an endless series of miracles, and the last miracle—for a handful of survivors—was liberation.

When I returned home as a free man, friends and acquaintances often asked me, almost obtrusively, a hackneyed question, "How is it that you managed to survive Auschwitz?" This question has always given me trouble, almost out of shame. I am sometimes asked it even now, after so many years. I answered then and I still answer now: "I don't know how it happened. It seems to me that since a small number of survivors returned, someone had to be among them. It turned out that I was one of them. That's all. I see no other explanation."

I did answer one woman somewhat differently, but it was only because she asked this question with clear resentment in her voice: "So many people died, but you survived. How did you do it?" I flushed, felt guilty, and blurted out, though not without some affectation, "I'm very sorry . . . I didn't do it on purpose . . ."

✦   ✦   ✦

Toward the end of 1943—I had then been in the camp for more than a year and a half—the camp authorities for the first time gave the Jewish prisoners permission to send their families one postcard. (Non-Jews had the right to regular correspondence and received food packages.) Each of us was given one such card to send.

We were given to understand that this was not so much "permission" as an official order, whose execution would be scrupulously observed and noncompliance severely punished. And what it meant in the camp "to be punished," we all knew very well. The cards were supposed to be filled out and turned in the next day before the morning roll call.

Animated consultations took place in small groups on what we should do. To write to our families meant to betray their place of residence, or rather hiding place, and tracking them down was unquestionably the goal of this supposed favor on the part of the authorities. Not to write at all was out of the question—that meant certain death. So most of the prisoners decided to address their cards to imaginary persons at random addresses. Others carried out the order exactly, assuming that it was a strategic trick by the Germans to show the world that the Jewish deportees were well and working normally.

The content of our cards was to include a few words about one's good state of health, something about good working conditions, no request for money or packages, and the address of the sender, stipulated to be "*Arbeitslager* Birkenau bei Neuberun," that is, Work Camp in Birkenau. We already knew that our real address was Work and Extermination Concentration Camp Auschwitz II–Birkenau.

I was completely at a loss. When I was deported from France, my brothers and their families were in the *zone libre* (free zone), which was now completely occupied by the German army. I also did not know whether they had changed their address since that time, or whether they had made their way to some other country. On the other hand, I could not simply give up this very uncertain but sole opportunity of trying to inform my family that I was alive and not suffering the worst conditions.

After much thought and weighing of the pros and cons, I decided to write to Polish friends (Aryans) residing in Paris, "I am sound and healthy and working in my profession." Besides, at that time this was the truth. Since I am a composer and violinist by profession, I wanted in this way to let them know that I was not badly off and that I had an easy job. I hoped that my friends would somehow be able to pass this "good news" along to my family.

When I returned to Paris after liberation, I found out that the card had reached the addressees rather quickly and that they had gotten it to my family. But no one believed that I was "working in my profession." Everyone thought that I had written this only to reassure them about my fate. Although almost nobody in 1942–43 could imagine what a Nazi concentration camp was like, no one was so naive as to believe that the Hitlerites had deported me in order to play the violin and compose music for them.

Today—after so many years, after so many more or less superficially read books, after documentary and feature films seen with reluctance, after so many oral depositions—people who know the camps only from hearsay are just as stubborn in accepting "how it really was there." Having accepted it, though, they return to their normal business as though nothing had happened. It was, it's over, there's nothing to talk about.

Like most former camp inmates I avoid talks on these subjects as much as possible, for I get the impression that, except for the "initiated," I am talking with people who do not understand the language I am speaking to them. And when circumstances come up in which I have to mention the orchestra that played in Auschwitz and my role in it, my interlocuters look at me in disbelief, almost like at someone not in his right mind.

"What do you mean? Music in Auschwitz? What for? And what did you play there? Surely only funeral marches?"

I am sometimes asked similar questions even now, in 1978! No, we did not play funeral marches. On the contrary, the marches we played—and about which I will say more later—were gay, lively, joyous, varied, and their role was to encourage work and the joy of life in the name of the camp slogan *Arbeit macht frei* (Work makes man free).

The first ambition of the *Lagerführer* (commander) of every camp worthy of the name was to form his own *Lagerkapelle* (camp musical group), whose main role was to ensure the flawless functioning of camp discipline and on occasion to afford our guardian angels a bit of entertainment and relaxation, so necessary in carrying out their not always appreciated work.

As I have said, to write about music in Auschwitz without sketching the general background against which it was played would be counter to the aim of this book. So I have to say something about this background, and from time to time it will be necessary for me to return to it.

◆   ◆   ◆

Auschwitz was a certain kind of "negative" world to which we were abducted. White became black and black, white; values were turned around 180 degrees. To put it more emphatically, every one of us had one of two possibilities before him: either to beat and torture his neighbors or to be beaten and tortured by them. Feelings of dignity and humanity were regarded as an offense; logical reasoning, as a sign of madness; compassion, as a sign of pathological psychic and moral weakness. On the other hand, the basest human instincts, previously tempered by education and culture, changed into genuine camp virtues, becoming one of the necessary—but not sufficient—conditions for survival.

So those who had the reputation of being the camp aristocrats were in fact common criminals, professional felons, bandits, safecrackers—in other words, the dregs of normal society. On the other hand, intellectuals, scientists, priests, rabbis, Jehovah's Witnesses, artists (with the exception of musicians, who "had it made")—all of these sank to the bottom of this new society of *Untermenschen* (submen) conceived by the Nazi genius.

Hundreds, thousands of deportees could not endure this sudden passage from one world to another, an antipodal one whose existence they could not have imagined in their most nightmarish hallucinations. Such people, after a few days, sometimes after a few hours, in the camp, "went to the wires," which in camp lingo meant to throw oneself onto the electrified high-tension barbed wires that separated us in a dense ring from neighboring camps and the outside world. In this way they avoided the experiences that befell the less "nervous" prisoners.

Less nervous ones. Like me. I came out with my life. To what do I owe this? I did not have to get rid of a single ordinary human virtue, and yet I survived. For me there is no doubt that I owe this to an unending series of miracles, but also, and perhaps above all, to my encounter with a few countrymen with a human face and a human heart. And there was frightfully little of this. Around us, among the prisoners, was being waged an incessant, desperate struggle for animal existence, for a piece of bread, a cigarette butt, a razor blade, an aspirin, a needle and thread, a sip of drinking water.

My "miracles" did not appear at once; I was not received with bread and salt. During the first weeks I lived in a complete daze, which accompanied a vain effort to get rid of all scruples and principles, to make myself like the ones who had done this and whom I did not stop envying.

The first of my miracles put me in the category of prisoners who occupied a "better" position in the camp hierarchy, at least for long enough to get better nourishment, to accumulate reserves in my organism, and to confront the last, darkest hours of my exile.

I was helped in this by . . . music. And so many times I had been told that one could not survive by music.

✦   ✦   ✦

I will not describe the circumstances in which I was arrested or the conditions in which my "resettlement" by the occupier took place. The only reality of this seventy-two-hour trip was the unimaginable crush of deportees in cattle cars and the hallucinations caused by an impossible-to-satisfy thirst.

From this trip only one memory is still vivid in my mind. At a certain moment I managed to push my way through the wall of human bodies to a small, grated window, the only one for the entire car, in order to try to get a bit of fresher air. The train was just slowing down and soon stopped before a building that resembled a railway station. The short distance made it possible for me to read the sign above, the name of the place . . .

Many years before this, when I was in Vienna, I found myself in front of the house in which Beethoven had died. I stood there for quite some time and read over and over, word for word, the inscription on the plaque, which said that in this house the composer Ludwig van Beethoven had died on 26 March 1827. Moved as never before, I thought that I would also like to see the house in Leipzig where Johann Sebastian Bach had ended his life.

And now my wish was fulfilled in a strange way, in the opposite direction, one might say. The town before whose railway station the train had stopped was called . . . Eisenach. And it was in Eisenach that Johann Sebastian Bach was born on 21 March 1685.

Such was my first encounter with music in the time of my resettlement.

✦   ✦   ✦

Most of the publications that discuss the psychological side of Nazi concentration camp experiences describe the first impres-

sion of the newly arrived prisoners as a "shock," "jolt," "bewil-
derment," and so on. These terms cannot be rejected or questioned, if only because there are no others. I am not sure
whether anyone would accept them who tasted in full the
Auschwitz existence and later wished to describe this first moment "in his own words." Not six but "Millions of Characters
in Search of an Author" could be the title of Pirandello's play
had he lived in the age of the Hitlerite extermination camps. I
have talked with many of my camp colleagues about this, and
nearly all of them rejected both "shock" and "jolt"—and any
other verbal expression at all. This was supposedly our experi-
ence, but at the same time it was not this at all. But what?

So far I have not been able to re-create this moment,
though I have tried very hard. Perhaps it is a question of memory, which fades; recollections, which deceive. In any case, as
far as I am concerned, the slender fragments of memory make
up a hazy impression, as though this collision with camp life
had plunged me into a lethargic stupor and at the same time as
though I had been shot from a catapult to another planet. One
thing I remember perfectly: the first questions I asked myself
were, What kind of a world is this? What sort of creatures are
those zebralike beings with shaved heads, some athletic, stout,
others infirm, swaying on their feet, emaciated like skeletons?

I tried to shake off this nightmare, to tell myself that it was
a dream, but an awakening did not come. What did come,
though, was a swift, abrupt answer to all questions.

I no longer had a first and last name: I had become a number, like Jean Valjean in *Les Misérables.* My identity was number 49,543 tattooed on my left forearm for the rest of my life, or
for what was left of it. After three days of endless "formalities"
and arduous training in forming up in groups of fives, paid for
with a hail of clubs, injuries, and sometimes the immediate

execution of the less apt pupils, they gave us bowls of some suspicious liquid, but hot and blissfully moistening our throats and entrails, dried out for days. Then they subjected us to symbolic ablutions under an icy shower, but since it was July we accepted this willingly. The same treatment awaited us in the winter, with temperatures of twenty degrees below zero, but for now we knew nothing about that.

All of this took place under the very "active" supervision of our brothers, comrades in adversity, who had succeeded in gaining higher positions and thereby had become our bosses. They drove us into a building that could have been a stable or cow shed but for the fact that no horse or cow or any larger animal could fit inside. Dogs could have, though, but this was not a place for dogs. It was reserved for creatures that resembled but were not people. These were the quarters for Jews.

The room was filled with a seemingly endless number of three-tiered bunks, in which one could fit only in a reclining position, head to the front, except for the upper bunk, in which a kneeling position was also possible. They drove us inside like useless cattle, ordered us to lie down in fives on each bunk, their cudgels incessantly raining down on us. Like scraps of food to animals in a cage they threw us striped jackets, pants, caps—nothing but rags. The confusion that resulted from this "cannot be described." So let us not describe it. Let us pass to the time when I could finally lie down, stretch out, straighten my numb limbs, try to drop off into a dream that would separate me from this reality that was another dream.

It was probably late evening, but I could not fall asleep. Hostility between neighbors of the same pallet was dreadfully human and understandable. One got in the way of another; each one took up more space than he supposedly should have. I curled up as much as I could, which enabled me to gain the good graces of my neighbors, and somehow settled down to longed-for sleep.

Suddenly I jumped up, hitting my head against the boards of the upper bunk. I thought I had heard something like rifle shots near by.

"What's that?" I asked one of my neighbors, who apparently was somewhat familiar with camp routine.

"What should it be? Nothing. They're shooting at someone who was going to the wires."

"If he was going to the wires, he would have been killed anyway, so why shoot?"

"You're stupid. If someone manages to get to the wires, he'll become so tangled up in them that to get him out will be no easy job, sometimes they have to shut off the current, and that's not so simple. But this way, a bullet in the head and it's taken care of. Do you get it?"

I got it. I now heard some other sounds in the distance, completely different ones, very strange, but they reminded me of something. Neither bangs nor strokes, rhythmical, hollow sounding, regular. Three close together, two further apart, three close together, two further apart . . . Their regularity rocked me off to blessed sleep.

✦   ✦   ✦

How many hours had I slept? Two? Five? Half an hour? I was wrenched from the abyss of nothingness by a terrible racket that rose up against the background of the guttural yelling of the floggers and the long-drawn-out moans of the flogged. Athletes in stripes were belaboring us with cudgels, yelling for the very pleasure of yelling: *Los! Aufstehen! Raus! Aber schnell!* (Come on! Get up! Out! Quickly!) We jumped up in unison from our pallets—we did not need to get dressed for we had not taken our clothes off—we bumped into one another; heads knocked against each other like billiard balls; with difficulty we fended off the shower of blows coming from all sides.

With the last glimmers of my reason I tried to understand why our comrades in misery, who were dressed in the same stripes as we were, perhaps only better fitting and less torn, were beating us with such conviction. I found no answer. The answer came after weeks, months. They were beating us so that they themselves would not be beaten. They thought that by beating us they would escape extermination. And some of them would survive, but others would be killed by the stronger and more resourceful.

From time to time I break off writing and wonder whether I should not spare the reader a description of some of the more painful fragments of this strange chronicle from another world. I may decide to leave one thing out; concerning another I hesitate and finally reluctantly decide to include it, since it seems to me, correctly or incorrectly, that the main theme of the story would lose its suggestiveness or even be incomprehensible without this. So please have a little more patience, for soon we will sail out into more expansive waters and breathe—*toutes proportions gardées*—a bit of fresher air.

◆　　　　◆　　　　◆

They drove us outside and, using their trusty cudgels, tried to form us up in rows of five so that the esmen* could as quickly as possible and with no mistake make a numerical count of every formation. Could anything be simpler than forming up in

* Camp slang for SS men.

fives, *zu fünfe!* This seemed like child's play, but not in reality. The blows they generously belabored us with made the task even more difficult. For some unknown reason suddenly in one row there were only four, and this "hole" had to be filled as quickly as possible; someone from the next row had to do it. But who? Two rushed forward at the same time. Now instead of the required five we had six before us, and behind them again only four. This game went on for at least an hour. Day was slowly beginning to dawn. No one knew what time it was. Three o'clock? Four? It was drizzling.

One more exercise awaited us, in comparison with which the previous one really was child's play. This was the collective, ceremonial, synchronized (ideally) saluting at the command of our fellow prisoner-executioners. This was a real art, and more than one paid with his life for the inability to learn it.

This art consisted of four successive stages, though there were only two commands: 1. *Mützen ab!* 2. *Mützen auf!* or "Caps off," "Caps on." But each command was divided into two separate tempos, hence the four stages and the strict, irrevocable protocol connected with them:

1. *Mützen* . . . The right hands rose up to the caps and waited motionlessly . . .

2. . . . *ab!* . . . hands snatched off the caps and with a synchronous, loud clap like the crack of a whip, slapped them against the right thighs.

3. *Mützen* . . . Hands went up, clumsily set caps on heads, and again waited . . .

4. . . . *auf!* . . . hands went down, this time without the caps, palms slapping against the right thighs with the same synchronous and loud-as-possible crack.

Only then could one freely adjust one's cap to be ready for a repetition of the ritual.

Try this on several hundred worn-out, starving, thirsty human beings hardly standing on their feet and you can imagine how much time it takes to learn this art, or rather to learn it imperfectly.

We were still being ordered about by our fellow prisoners in stripes. So far the esmen in camp had not done us the least harm. They were faultlessly relieved of this task by our comrades, who knows whether with better result. The moment came, however, when even they felt tired—not so much they as their throats. For the moment, they interrupted the drill, and the command was given: *Rührt euch* (at ease)!

In the meantime the day had begun to peer lazily from behind the leaden clouds. We gladly took advantage of the fact that no one was paying attention to us and sat down on the bare, moist earth to take a breather. I looked around on all sides. The camp was gradually coming to life. Specters in stripes floated by like shadows, now at a brisk pace, now at a run, in various directions. A small group was moving down the main road, groaning under the weight of smoking barrels furnished with iron rings. Through these rings were long poles that rested on the backs of the carriers. The barrels probably contained the liquid concoction to which we had recently been treated.

Teenagers, premature dregs of society, ran lengthways and crosswise about the area with some papers in their hands, apparently instructions from the camp authorities for the prisoner-guards. Before one of the barracks—which we would soon learn to call "blocks"—a small group of inert, skeleton-like creatures, former people dressed in rags or befouled shirts, had settled down. Others were naked, holding their heads in their hands. I was told that these were the sick, waiting to be sent to the hospital.

It was getting lighter all the time. This allowed me to witness a bizarre event. One of the barrels slipped with a crash from the poles holding it, and all of the boiling water spilled out on the road. The carriers raised an inhuman shout, whether from the burns they received or from the blows from the cudgels of the *Vorarbeiter** who had run up, it is hard to say. Probably one and the other. I turned my eyes in another direction, in the faint and completely unfounded hope that I would see something less depressing.

My hope turned out to be less faint than I had expected. As in a theater or cinema there was a radical change of scenery. So radical that at first I did not believe my eyes.

Also moving down the main road, but much closer to the entrance gate, was a small group of prisoners dressed in the same stripes as we, loaded down with strange equipment whose form seemed very familiar to me, but precisely because it was familiar I simply refused to believe that this equipment was what I took it for. Could it be? . . . No, this was impossible, these were illusions, hallucinations bordering on professional delusion. And yet . . .

In a state of highest excitement I followed every movement of the men carrying these strange and yet very familiar objects. Now, when they had been set up vertically, at the proper distance from each other, with small tables before each of them, my doubts vanished, yielding to new stupefaction. These were music stands! Made from roughly hewn wood, awkward, misshapen, but real music stands!

* Supervisors of smaller work parties.

The guttural shout *Achtung!* wrenched me from stupefaction and disbelief. I mindlessly aped the others and only after a few minutes became aware that we were once again going through the arduous drill of taking off and putting on our caps. This time the exercise was somewhat briefer, not because we did it better but because the ceremonial of morning roll call was to take place in a moment under the watchful supervision of the *Blockführer,* * with the practical application of the lesson of "fives" in every row.

I was only half-present at this ghastly ceremony in which I was taking part for the first time. My mind followed with difficulty the mechanically performed gestures. The music stands and tables I had seen a moment ago gave me no peace, they transported me to spheres so remote from this nightmare that surrounded me. I concentrated and tried to reason—as though reason was of any use here. Music stands were for music scores, and scores—were music. Who played here? The executioners or their victims? And what did they play here? The dance of skeletons? Nazi hymns? Funeral marches?

◆　　　　◆　　　　◆

After roll call they drove us back into our kennel. A new order was given: "Sew on the numbers!" What numbers? Sew them on where? Soon all was clear. They meant the number that was branded on our left forearm. But where could we get a needle, thread, a pencil, a piece of cloth?

My nervousness turned out to be unnecessary. Everything had been foreseen. Specialists in this rite were waiting for us at

* An SS man in charge of several barracks.

the barracks. In exchange for a piece of bread, a portion of margarine or marmalade, they sewed on the number for you in the right place—on the left side of the chest—a nicely printed number, and beside it they drew two opposite triangles, one yellow, one pink, making up a "disgraceful" mark, the six-branched Star of David. These were not official tailors, but tailors out of choice and inventiveness. There were not many of them; they plied this "trade" because they knew that the newly arrived deportees would not be able to manage on their own and were thus at their mercy. This was a small omen of the barter on a large scale that I would encounter as time went on and I slowly became familiar with my new environment, its customs and laws.

The entire day up to evening roll call passed in these tailoring activities, interspersed with fights and haggling over every gram of bread. Finally, I could lie down in my doghouse and try to separate myself in thought from the rest of the world. One thing was dreadfully clear to me: I was in a trap from which there was no escape, unless it was to the other world. I looked around at my neighbors, wretches like me. That was how creatures looked today who not long ago were people, had families, friends, worked, looked with hope to a bright, promising future. The war was raging in the world, things were happening, people were fighting for the victory of good over evil. But we here . . .

A shot rang out, a second one, a third one . . . To be sure, I could "go to the wires." So not everything was lost. Maybe tomorrow, maybe the day after that; we would see. Temporarily my attention was again attracted to the rhythmical beats I had heard before, three close together, two further apart, three close together, two further apart . . . Now I knew: these were the beats of a big bass drum, part of an orchestra. I could not hear it, for the sound of the drum drowned it out. So there was an orchestra here. The matter of the music stands had been explained.

◆   ◆   ◆

Later I was sent to work. I went out with the detachment in the morning and returned in the evening. Going and coming to the sounds of march music, which I did not hear because I did not want to. I will not describe this "work" because I am in a hurry to get to music, the main subject of my book. Except that with every day—I felt this almost physically—the pounds were coming off me one after another, and how many I had left I had no idea. In any case, some adequate minimum, for after twenty days of this convict's regime I was still alive.

One evening, like every evening, I was lying on my pallet wondering how much longer I would last. Homebred statistics said that, on the average, a prisoner could last six weeks—unless before this he preferred "to go to the wires." So I still had three weeks before me . . . Eternity. Those merciful wires gave me no peace, like an irresistible temptation. To go? Not to go?

No! I won't go to the wires. In any case, not right away. I'll go when I can't hold out any longer. Maybe something, maybe someone . . .

What happened next I never stop comparing with the scene in which Faust, instead of drinking the cup of poison, calls Mephistopheles to save his lost soul and restore his youth and joy of life.

My hopeless whispering "maybe something, maybe someone" turned out to be a magic incantation. With the difference that, instead of Mephistopheles, my savior in spite of himself appeared as though from out of the ground, the first miracle in a long series of miracles that kept me alive and ultimately restored my freedom.

My benefactor was the barracks chief. Tall, broad-shouldered, a real athlete, he stood as though on purpose beside my bunk and in a stentorian voice called out in Polish,

"Is there someone here who speaks Polish and plays bridge?"

I almost failed to understand what he meant, but instinctively I stopped munching on my bread, jumped down from the bunk, and stood before him at attention.

"Come on!"

There were no other candidates. As I learned later, my transport, which had come from France, included very few people who spoke Polish. So to some extent I was Fortune's darling.

A few minutes later, dirty, unshaven, not believing my eyes and ears, I was sitting at a bridge table in the private room of the barracks chief, in the company of two other VIPs in striped clothing, and playing one rubber after another like an equal with equals. Those two mates were also barracks chiefs, in other barracks. They gathered every evening for a bit of relaxation after a hard day's work. When you think that each of them had battered, often to death, several inmates—not for nothing, since it allowed them to appropriate their food rations—they certainly deserved a rest. That evening their usual fourth for bridge was preoccupied with receiving new victims to his barracks, and to this I owed the honorable role that had befallen me: that of worthy partner to a man who tomorrow might turn out to be my executioner. Fate had it that my potential murderer became my savior. I know his name, but I will not mention it. If he is still alive, may the rest of his life pass "as on a broad field, sweetly and happily." And if he is not alive, may the soil over him be light.

During one of the hands we played, I managed to mutter to him that I was a violinist and composer. He looked at me with a bitter, honest reproach.

"Why didn't you tell me this sooner? Tomorrow you'll stay in the barracks and I'll take you over to the orchestra."

A second companion added, choking with laughter, "And if you're accepted, maybe you'll live a little longer, ha, ha, ha!"

All three of them burst out laughing. Their merriment very nearly spread to me.

My benefactor did more for me than he promised. After the card game was over, he gave me a haircut and shave, had me wash up in a bowl of the hot concoction that had been served to us as "tea," and told me to report to him at dawn on the following day.

The very thought that tomorrow I would not leave the camp for work filled me with good cheer such as I had not known for a long time.

◆   ◆   ◆

The dazzling sight that spread before my eyes after crossing the threshold of Barracks 15 completely staggered me. My attention was first attracted, "professionally" one might say, by the wooden partition a few meters away on which were hanging all sorts of brass and woodwind instruments, everything polished to a bright shine. I distinguished in turn a huge tuba helicon, a trombone, a few trumpets, a brass tenor and alto horns, saxophones, clarinets, and two flutes, one a piccolo. Leaning against the wall in one of the corners was an impressive double bass with a bow stuck under the strings, in another a bass drum with cymbals and a snare drum with all of the percussion paraphernalia. On a wide, solid shelf specifically designed for this purpose were a few accordions and violins in cases. One of them, somewhat bigger than the others, probably contained a viola. I failed to see a violoncello. A second shelf, somewhat smaller, was filled with music scores and a pile of blank music paper.

Sitting at a large table in this neither hall nor vestibule were two men eating their breakfast. The smell of fried sausage with onions gave my palate exquisite torture. I licked my lips and waited. Paradoxically a verse of Pushkin's came to my mind: "What has the coming day in store for me?"

My angel—bridge player, who had conducted me here, walked up to the older man and, pointing to me, whispered something in his ear. He was unquestionably the conductor of the orchestra and had an engaging appearance, with kind-hearted eyes. At first he took me for a Frenchman, since he knew that my transport had come from France, but before long his face lit up when he learned that I was "really" a Pole and that he could speak to me in Polish. He gave me a violin and asked me to play something.

My fingers were stiff, bruised, my arms sore, the bow slipped out of my hand, but fortunately my left arm was almost sound. I thought it best to play something technically effective and, without reflection, I rushed into the first bars of Mendelssohn's concerto, completely forgetting that he was a Jewish composer and that the performance of his works was forbidden in Germany and in the occupied countries as well. Quite fortunately, after only a few bars the conductor gave me a sign to stop.

"Good. Technique not bad, not bad. Tell your barracks

chief that you have been accepted and for him to transfer you to this barracks. Also tell him to take you to the *Bekleidungskammer* [clothing storeroom], where they'll exchange those rags you're wearing for decent stripes. We're going out to play now, but in the meantime you can practice a bit outside, for your fingers are rather stiff. But tomorrow morning you'll go out with the rest of us."

My barracks chief turned out to be a man of his word. If he was supposed to kill someone, he did; if he was supposed to help, he helped to the very end. All of my registration and clothing matters were already taken care of. I looked fairly decent and had some time to limber up my fingers and bow arm with a few effective exercises. I could not do this in the barracks, for it would have disturbed the copyists. So I sat down on a hillock between our barracks and the next one and, ignoring the surprised and slightly derisive looks of the camp "aristocrats" passing by, enthusiastically ran through tiresome but practical exercises, scales and passages to restore my fingers to their former dexterity.

Before me rose an endless row of cement pillars whose tops were bent in my direction. These pillars were connected with parallel rows of electrified barbed wires, but the wires no longer tempted me. The violin I was holding would be my protective shield.

Somewhat further away was a second string of pillars, but bent in the opposite direction. Between the two was a road on which from time to time fully loaded carts moved lazily, pulled or pushed by striped cattle resembling human beings.

I continued to practice, telling myself that besides the violin and the orchestra nothing should concern me. But my eyes were attracted by strange creatures walking back and forth behind the second row of wires. What sort of creatures were they?

Human beings? Hobgoblins? Children? A few of them came up closer to the wires, and only then did I recognize them. These creatures, dressed in worn-out Soviet uniforms, with shaved heads and gray, gaunt faces—were women! Or rather, they had once been women. They saw me, exposed their emaciated arms and swollen legs and called out as though out of habit: *Brot! Brot!* (Bread!)

Suddenly the women vanished like specters. An esman had appeared on the road. He stopped and listened to my exercises through the wires. I jumped up, took off my cap according to regulations, and snapped to attention. The German made an encouraging motion with his hand: *Weiter machen* (go on). After that he left.

I returned to my exercises with redoubled energy.

◆   ◆   ◆

The camp seemed almost deserted. The detachments had probably long since gone out to work. Sudden fear came over me on account of my loneliness. My fingers were still stiff, a pain in my right shoulder was troubling me. I decided to go back to the barracks to see what was going on there, what the musicians did after they came back from playing.

I now found three men instead of two. All three were busy writing or perhaps copying music. The instruments were hanging on their pegs as they had been that morning, as though no one had touched them in the meantime. But where were the musicians? I timidly asked the conductor.

"What do you mean, where? They're gone out with the detachments to work!"

I was bathed in sweat.

"With which detachments?" I moaned with my heart in

my mouth. The answer came from the director's companion, a sickly looking gentleman who apparently had a fine sense of humor.

"What does it matter to you, with which ones? You'll soon go straight to the *Himmelkommando* anyway!"

"Himmelkommando" . . . that meant straight to heaven. No one laughed. The conductor kept on writing. The third person, a quiet, kindly, dark-haired man, looked at me meaningfully, as though telling me not to worry.

This look turned out to be prophetic: the one who in the end went to the *Himmelkommando* was the one who was sending me there today. Since in a certain sense he is one of the leading characters of this story, let me introduce the reader at once, in anticipation of events, to this entire trio:

Jan Zaborski was conductor of the band and also the tuba player. The unpleasant Franz Kopka was a drummer and also kapo of the band. And the dark-haired man with the prophetic look was Ludwik Żuk-Skarszewski, violinist, clarinetist, copyist-arranger and . . . my future second deliverer.

✦   ✦   ✦

I had such stage fright as though I were about to perform as a soloist before a large audience of music experts and critics. The orchestra in full assembly drew up in the required fives in the main lane, opposite our barracks, quite a distance from the podium to which we would shortly direct our steps. To my great surprise and also consternation, at the head of the group was Franz Kopka, holding the conductor's baton with an expression of triumph, while Zaborski, the official conductor, took his position at the very rear with the helicon on his back. In the first row I saw a few trumpeters, behind them tenor, alto, and baritone horns, accordions, clarinets, a saxophone, a snare drum, and a bass drum with cymbals. At the very end, just behind the tuba, stood the violinists—I among them—holding closed cases under their arms because they could not play on the march.

Kopka gave the command *Vorwärts! Marsch!* and the title of the march we were supposed to play. At the same time, the snare drum beat out a few rhythmical measures, which were soon joined by the ear-splitting crash of the bass drum and cymbals, all of this in order to make us march in perfect step. The sounds of a noisy, lively march rang out, and the column moved in close order toward the gate of the camp. By the gate was a stage, already set up with music stands, where the real performance of our group would take place.

Along the way we were joyously greeted by the kapos, who were busy forming up their detachments for a perfect march out. After a few minutes we found ourselves beside the stage. Kopka interrupted the playing and brought the column to a halt, energetically raising and lowering his baton. The musicians scurried off to their places and spread out their music on the stands; the violinists took their instruments out of their cases and tuned up, plucking the strings with their fingers.

I was ready to begin the first march and waited for the signal. But Kopka was in no hurry. He was in a fine humor and shouted out the name of a tango to the musicians. Except for me, all of them seemed accustomed to this ritual. It was still early, the detachments had not formed up yet, so why not make the waiting more pleasant?

Kopka put the baton aside and directed with two fingers of each hand, the index and middle fingers, all the time making supposedly amusing motions with his whole body and putting on the airs of a consummate artist. Fortunately the musicians did not pay the slightest attention to him or they would surely have lost the beat.

The guttural shout of the esmen coming from the watch-tower interrupted the drawn-out tango. Kopka rushed to the gate and stood at attention before one of the officers. After a while he ran back and gave a different group of musicians the name of another tango. The sounds of a popular jazz hit rang out, one that I had heard not long ago when I was still free. This time we played to the end, and the last chords were received with applause by the detachments standing near by.

A new guttural shout resounded: *Los! Musik!* Both sides of the gate swung open. The familiar tune blared forth of a march as old as the hills, "Alte Kameraden." At the same time, the individual detachments moved one after another in perfect ca-dence toward the exit, where a careful count was taken of each and the number of those leaving recorded. Upon return to the camp the number in each detachment had to agree exactly with the number recorded, for otherwise—heaven help us all!

I was appalled by the terrible playing out of tune of some of the wind instruments. The strings could not help, but fortu-nately the winds were drowned out by the powerful thumping of the bass drum and the simultaneous clashing of the brass cymbals. These were the same sounds that had come to me from far away during the first hours of my stay here.

The last detachment had left the camp. We packed up our instruments and formed up again in the main lane, but this time facing the opposite direction. The same ceremonial was repeated with the snare drum, the bass drum, cymbals, and once again there resounded the out-of-tune chords of a lively march that was to lead us back to the barracks. There each of us put his instrument in its proper place, after which all of the musicians went outside. I wondered where I should go and what I should do, to stay or go with the others. The shrill shout of Franz Kopka delivered me from my perplexity.

"*Raus!* Get out of here! To work! I don't want to see anyone here!"

Indeed, I did remember that Kopka had muttered something about work in some detachment that in the end could turn out to be a *Himmelkommando*. I "got out" as ordered. Outside, the rest of the musicians had already lined up obediently *zu fünfe*, ready to march out of the camp in conformity with the daily routine. The baritone player, who was the *Vorarbeiter* of the musicians' detachment, waited for me to join the others. We moved out for work, just as the rest of the camp had done. Except that no one played music for us.

Three privileged persons remained in the barracks: Zaborski, Kopka, and Żuk.

I will also not describe those days I spent in the double role of musician and galley slave. I'll just say that, although I did not know how long it would last, I did know that it could not last long.

We went out a little later than the normal detachments, right after playing the marches, and returned a little earlier in order to get back in time for the ceremonial of greeting the detachments returning from work. It may have been a psychological acoustical illusion, but it seemed to me that we played the evening marches in a somewhat slower tempo in order to keep pace with those who were returning. The people themselves not only walked slowly, heavily, but some of them dragged the inert bodies of the maimed, unconscious, or dead, who had to "return" to the camp for the numerical count to be taken again.

In the morning and evening was music; in the meantime, hard labor diversified only by the blows showered on us by our fellow prisoners, not only when some esman passed by but also for no reason at all, as a symbol of the might of power, art for art's sake, to give themselves importance and a feeling of their own usefulness. To this was added gnawing hunger, which could not be satisfied or even slightly appeased by the theoretical liter of "soup" given out during the one-hour break around noon. And the burning thirst. Even inside the camp it could not be quenched, since the water in Birkenau was somehow "copperized," with a strange, repulsive copper color; in any case, everyone knew that it was poison.

And every evening I asked myself the same obsessive question: how long could I last? I recalled the sinister giggling of my recent fellow bridge player: "If you're accepted, maybe you'll live a little longer."

A little longer. How long? A few hours? A few days? Weeks?

And now the next miracle happened: one morning—exactly one week after I had been accepted into the group—our musical detachment, after having played the required marches, was moving out of the camp with a cart fully loaded with coal, when Ludwik Żuk ran up from Barracks 15 and told the baritone *Vorarbeiter* that he was taking me back to the barracks because I had been appointed a *Notenschreiber*, a music copyist, and would not be going out to work any more.

To be sure, in the last few days I had had more than one opportunity to chat with Żuk about this and that, about our common misery and about music in general, and about how the group sounded. And I had reason to believe that in time the scraps of our conversations would give rise to, if not friendship, at least good comradeship. But could I imagine that this Żuk, in spite of Kopka, his superior, would use his Aryan connections and make energetic efforts to pull me out of the *Arbeits-*

kommando and have me officially assigned to the group of copyists?

He told me later that he had taken a liking to me right away, that he had recognized me as a "genuine musician," and that he had decided to do everything he could to draw me into working on music alone. And he did so.

Zaborski accepted my nomination with his typical kindliness and even, I might say, with ill-concealed satisfaction. I later found out from Żuk that Zaborski had been an organist in Biała Podlaska and had been sent to the camp for his part in making false identity papers and birth certificates for Jews. He was officially appointed *Kapellmeister* (conductor) of the orchestra, but Kopka took advantage of his goodness and resourcelessness to move into first place, in which he was helped by his alleged German nationality. (No one knew by what twist of fate Kopka, who was actually half-Polish and half-Czech, appeared on the list of prisoners as a full-blooded German.) Kopka, as I had foreseen, was now filled with even greater hatred for me than he had shown before. I must admit that it was entirely mutual. Except that he did not hide his hatred for me, whereas I had to hate in silence and submissiveness.

Ludwik Żuk-Skarszewski had been arrested along with several other professors for "clandestine teaching" and had been sent to Auschwitz I on 3 June 1942 (hardly a month and a half before my arrival in Birkenau) with the number 37,939. In this proto-Auschwitz, which had been established in June 1940, a large orchestra had existed for quite some time under the direction of Franz Nierychło, a Silesian, who was at the same time—for what reason is a mystery, such were the oddities of camp life—the chief, that is, kapo, of the prisoners' kitchen. After having received his proper share of physical torments, Żuk got into the orchestra as a violinist. Shortly thereafter Nierychło was ordered by the authorities to take sixteen musicians to Birkenau, whose commander also wanted to have his own *Lagerkapelle*. Among these sixteen was my future friend Żuk.

◆   ◆   ◆

Our group slowly but constantly grew larger. Day after day trains were disgorging onto the Auschwitz railway ramp thousands of Jews from all over Europe, only part of whom swelled the population of the camp, since most of them went straight to the gas chambers. Żuk did as much as he could to track down musicians among the doomed. Kopka did not protest, knowing that this was the commander's wish. So our numbers were increased with a few Frenchmen, a few Greeks, Jews from Poland and Germany, but mostly Dutchmen, who turned out to be excellent instrumentalists, virtuosos one could say. Of course, none of them spoke Polish, so another duty was thrust on me that had nothing to do with music.

For it turned out that besides Zaborski and Kopka, my two official superiors, I also had a third, very likely more dangerous than Kopka. This "third man" was Walerian Agdan, who played the accordion (out of tune) but who was also the *Stubendienst*, that is, the room supervisor, responsible for order in the barracks and the observance of official discipline. And since he wanted very much "for those foreign kikes to know" what he would beat them for, he came up with the idea of appointing me *Dolmetscher*, that is, translator of his orders to the musicians who did not know Polish.

With my knowledge of French, English, and German there would have been nothing alarming in this for me had it not been coupled with an incredible proviso: for unsatisfactory compliance with these orders, for any violation of discipline whatsoever, it was *I* who would be punished and not the "foreign kikes," since any infraction unquestionably meant that I had been remiss in my role as *Dolmetscher*. The punishment would be measured out with a certain number of cudgel blows on the rump, proportionate to the degree of the offense.

My greatest nightmare was the bedspreads, or rather blankets, we had been issued and which, after reveille, had to be folded in a special, impeccable way, strictly according to the regulations. These light-brown blankets with the ghastly emblem of the Waffen SS were notorious for their obstinacy and recalcitrance, which could be overcome only with the greatest difficulty. And when an inspection by the *Blockführer* was announced, more than one musician preferred to sleep on the floor rather than disturb the perfect folds of the blankets so arduously arranged the day before.

I must admit that Agdan never punished me for "blanket" infractions, for he was probably aware that they had nothing to do with my role as translator. But for other types of violations his cudgel reached me two times in all, not because the "foreign kikes" had misunderstood me but because I had misunderstood Agdan's street slang.

These incidents, which were fortunately rather infrequent, only slightly disturbed my musical collaboration with Żuk. I slowly returned to tolerable physical condition, even though the food had not improved one iota. But no longer having to perform convict's labor outside the camp restored more strength to me that the most plentiful nourishment.

Kopka left me pretty much alone, not out of conviction or out of a change in attitude, but because he had to. The influx of new, excellent musicians created a situation with which neither Zaborski, who was often ill, nor especially the ignoramus

Kopka could cope. Except for a few continually repeated marches, the orchestra had no music, and our commander, *Hauptsturmführer* Johann Schwarzhuber, who, as it turned out, was a great music lover, constantly insisted on expanding the repertoire, both of marches and of light music. Time and again another esman, the commander's emissary, brought us the "bare" melody of a new march or some popular piece that had to be harmonized, orchestrated for a larger group, and transcribed for individual parts as quickly as possible. Kopka was well aware that he could not cope with this alone and that to a large extent his position as kapo of the band would depend on the efficiency of the arranger-copyists, hence also on me. He only knew how to transcribe music, and so at most he could copy already written violin parts, and even then only in a small amount. Hence his role in preparing the scores was minor.

Zaborski, whose health continued to decline, was almost incapable of any work and barely shuffled along with his helicon behind the marching band. Soon, utterly exhausted, he went to the *Krankenhaus* (hospital) and died there in November 1942. So now the real responsibility for the orchestra material fell on Żuk and me, with the tacit consent of Kopka.

✦   ✦   ✦

My collaboration with Żuk did not last long. In October 1942 he was transported back to Auschwitz I, where he and a few other Poles were given the death sentence in retaliation for the blowing up a German ammunition train going to the front, a sabotage that took place in Pionki near Radom. This sentence applied to all political prisoners who came from the incriminated district. At the last moment, when the list of the condemned men was checked, it turned out that Żuk was from the district of Lemberg (Lvov). Hence he escaped death, thanks to the proverbial German scrupulousness.

At this point our recollections differ. After so many years what is strange about that? As far as I remember, soon after he returned to Birkenau, Żuk came down with typhoid fever and was taken to the *Krankenbau*. After a few weeks, news reached me of his death. In the first letters I received from him after we had reestablished contact, he said that he had returned to the orchestra and had played in it until March 1943, when he was transferred to the Gross-Rosen concentration camp. "And so," he wrote to me, "I took my leave of the orchestra. I remember my march out of Birkenau, when you looked at me sadly from the podium of the *Lagerkapelle*, and this picture has remained forever in my memory."

So it was I who was in error. This is one of the most pleasant errors I have ever made in my life.

◆   ◆   ◆

Zaborski's departure caused great confusion among the musicians. Despite his apparently weak character, he had enjoyed unquestioned authority among us all and, unlike other VIPs, had never injured anyone merely for the pleasure of doing injury. He had treated me with courtesy and even with esteem, as a "colleague." I felt his loss especially painfully, since it was closely linked with my future destiny.

As I had instinctively foreseen, Kopka did not hesitate to take advantage of the situation and imperiously nominated himself *Kapellmeister*, for which, as a supposed *Reichsdeutsch* (Aryan German), he received the approval of the authorities. He probably thought that waving a baton was a snap and that he could do it no worse than Zaborski or anyone else.

In any case, Kopka's self-nomination gave me the shivers. For a long time I had known that he hated me and that he was also aware of my feelings for him. I was sure that his first move would be not only to kick me out of the group of copyists but to kick me out of the orchestra as well and to send me to some hard-labor detachment.

Things turned out quite differently, however.

Having found himself at the head of a group that now numbered more than thirty persons, Kopka immediately realized that the job was beyond him. Apart from the conducting itself, it was necessary to prepare new instrumental materials on the spur of the moment, that is, harmonize and orchestrate new pieces every now and again, transcribe the individual parts, and compose new marches in the German style or recreate old ones from memory in accordance with the wishes of the commander or his subordinates. For the time being I was the only one who could do this job, as Kopka was well aware. This led to a tacit agreement between us that was beneficial to both sides: Kopka gathered in the laurels thanks to my work and knowledge, while I could quietly stay in the barracks and find an outlet for my energy and perhaps a bit of forgetfulness in pseudo-creative musical activity.

Kopka's role as *Notenschreiber* was limited to copying some of the parts I had arranged. In no way did this diminish his authority in his own eyes. He had a tailor fashion a black silk armband with a finely embroidered silver lyre, the symbol of music, and showed it off at the head of the orchestra, waving his baton, to which no one paid any attention. He also enlisted for himself a cook's boy, a violinist newly arrived from Poland, who served up tasty dishes for him with sausage, margarine, potatoes, onions, and garlic. None of us had any idea where Kopka got these priceless treasures. One thing we did know was that every few days he left the barracks for half an hour or an hour and came back either loaded down with provisions or empty-handed, glum and angry at everything and everybody.

✦   ✦   ✦

Relentless camp reality clouded this make-believe atmosphere, however, everyday raking in a harvest of death among the prisoners and among the musicians as well. Apart from a few privileged persons, everyone went out to work just as before and returned in a state of extreme physical and mental exhaustion. Some managed to endure this, while others broke down completely. Some threw themselves on the wires. The size of the orchestra changed almost from day to day and in time shrank catastrophically. Things got so bad that one day Agdan sailed into me with a threat,

"You, *Dolmetscher*, tell those bastards that if they don't stop going to the wires, I'll kill them like dogs!"

However, I succeeded, not without difficulty, in explaining to him that it would be better to lose a few musicians than the entire orchestra, whose core and best element was the "foreign kikes."

Indeed, Walerian Agdan was a strange character. His sly pockmarked face, with its slanted eyes and pointed nose, breathed with hatred for man in general and for Jews in particular. He not only accepted the German racist theory as gospel but applied it more zealously than many a Hitlerite. At the same time, though, there glowed in his soul a strange spark of misconceived patriotism addressed to the Polish Jews. When in the winter of 1942 we were given sweaters and earmuffs, the Polish Jews were the only ones who, along with the other Poles, scorned earmuffs. They stood during roll call with uncovered ears, while the Jews from other countries, Frenchmen, Greeks, Dutchmen, beat their thighs, sides, and covered ears to warm up. On one especially frosty morning I heard Agdan's voice behind me addressing a neighbor,

"Look how our Polish kikes are not afraid of the frost and look at those foreign pansies."

The routine inside and outside the camp continued to decimate the ranks of the orchestra, however. The musicians continued to fall sick and went to the hospital, to the gas chamber, or to the wires. Others took their place. The sudden changes in the size of our group created a situation for which I was completely unprepared. The sudden disappearance of one or a few musicians caused empty spaces in the chords, quite often in the solo parts. This imposed on me the gloomy obligation of carefully observing the physical and mental health of my less hardy colleagues.

I was also forced to make use of a special kind of orchestration, called *odeon* in musical slang, which makes it possible for any group to perform any work, regardless of the presence or absence of one or even a few musicians. This is achieved by writing the most important themes in small notes in the other parts, so that if the main soloist is absent he can be replaced by someone else who plays these small notes instead. In time I gained real mastery in this strange art, and the "holes" in the group's sound that had bothered me appeared less and less often. Only after long months did the makeup of the orchestra, which became ever larger, stabilize somewhat, allowing me to abandon the trade of musical gravedigger.

✦   ✦   ✦

Though my relations with Kopka had generally improved, our "cooperation" was filled with incidents of various kinds, sometimes amusing, sometimes unpleasant, even menacing. One of them in particular stands out in my memory.

One day a messenger from the commander ran up with the score of a new march that was very popular in Germany, with orders to include it without delay in the repertoire. This march was called "Berliner Luft" or "Berlin Air." Fortunately, we had received another copyist in the person of Leon Weintraub, a Russian Jew from France, who played the saxophone and violin. Both of us copied the parts I had arranged, and in a few days the full orchestration of this march was ready.

At that time the *Sonderkommando* (special detachment) of sad memory, whose job consisted in handling and burning the corpses of those who had been gassed and which later was transferred to the closed area of the newly built crematorium, still resided inside Birkenau and went out to work like all the other detachments—to the encouraging sounds of our marches. Because of its continual contact with bodies that were often in a state of advanced decomposition, the *Sonderkommando* detachment gave off a terrible, choking stench as it marched out, a smell that did not dissipate for several minutes.

An ill-fated coincidence had it that we played "Berliner Luft" for the first time, the day after the orchestration had been completed, at the precise moment when the *Sonderkommando* was passing our podium on the way to the gate. The stench of bodies filled the entire camp. The orchestra, which was used to it, paid not the slightest heed and continued to play "Berliner Luft" under the devil-may-care baton of Kopka.

Suddenly from the esmen's watchtower we heard a shrill whistle and then the hoarse shout: *Kappelmeister!* Kopka ran up to the gate in a gentle trot and snapped to attention. One of the esmen led him inside the building, while another came over and told us to play another march. We instantly caught on to what was wrong. Berlin air and the air of the *Sonderkommando*—not a bad comparison! We feared some collective punishment, but what could we do? I waved the baton mechanically and conducted the new march to its conclusion.

Fifteen minutes later the *Kapellmeister* returned, white as chalk, swaying on his feet, with both hands glued to his buttocks. He had gotten twenty-five strokes. The authorities did not believe in the coincidence of the two "airs" and accused him of intentionally making a mockery of the capital of the Third Reich.

We had hardly returned to the barracks and put away our instruments when Kopka summoned me, ordered me to lean over, and gave me the same number of strokes. But since he was weakened and incapable of much physical effort, the retribution did not turn out to be very painful.

From then on we were very careful not to play "Berliner Luft" when the *Sonderkommando* was marching out.

❖   ❖   ❖

Leon Weintraub wrote music in a fine, legible hand. He was an average musician, poor saxophonist, but a nimble and brilliant violinist. His speciality was Gypsy romances and Russian folk music, both of which Kopka was wild about. Weintraub was perhaps the only musician for whom our *Kapellmeister* displayed a genuine liking, tinged with admiration. Weintraub was a man of athletic build and had a great gift for telling spicy romantic adventures, which he illustrated with suggestive drawings. Kopka repeatedly pulled him away from copying music to have him play a few of his favorite melodies on the violin or tell him some spicy story. In gratitude Kopka sometimes gave him the leftovers from his meal. He looked a bit askance at the excellent comradely and "professional" relations between me and his favorite. For Weintraub was a good friend of mine, and in addition, thanks to his collaboration with me, the music-copying output had risen considerably.

At about the same time as Weintraub arrived, we got an infusion of new blood, which in time filled in the catastrophic holes in our group. Then Heinz Lewin appeared among us, a personality who is worth saying a few words about, since in all of my life I have never met another musical phenomenon like him.

Born in eastern Germany in the town of Halle-an-der-Saale, he had been brought here as a German Jew from the French camp in Gurs (Pyrenees). He played the flute like a virtuoso and was just as good on the clarinet, saxophone, double bass, and other instruments; in other words, it would be quicker to mention the instruments he didn't play. But that's not all. He was also a violin maker, mechanic and . . . expert watchmaker! And it was this speciality that was to turn out to be his salvation, for he would not have endured more than two to three days of physical labor outside the camp. As I have mentioned, musicians like Lewin are as scarce as hen's teeth. This can be best seen in the confession he once made to me: "I always dreamed about playing in a group in which I would be the worst musician." Unfortunately, our group could in no way fulfill his wish.

On the lean side, frail, slightly stooped, Lewin was ideally suited for a sedentary life, which fortunately for him became his lot almost immediately after he landed in Birkenau. As soon as his watchmaking skills became known, he was showered from all sides—prisoners and esmen—with broken watches to be fixed, and from somewhere (from where we will see later) he was supplied with a complete arsenal of spare parts and precision tools: hands, faces, watchcases, cogged wheels, castellated nuts, going barrels, screwdrivers, tangs, gravers, chisels, watchmaker's glasses—in short, everything the heart of a watchmaker could desire. With the consent of the authorities, Lewin was placed at a separate table, which he hardly ever left, except for rare occasions when a solo musician had to be replaced.

A watch in the camp was an important distinction, honor, almost a badge of merit. A watch meant a high position in the camp hierarchy and in a certain sense secure settlement on one of its levels. All of the kapos, *Vorarbeiter*, barracks chiefs—all camp VIPs wore watches on their wrists. All of the esmen too, of course. And since both one and the other did not cease to belabor their victims with blows, with either the fist or the forearm, it is no wonder that the watches of the "propertied classes" were always getting broken, damaged, or crushed to a pulp. So Lewin had his hands full. From dawn to dusk he sat bent over the table with a watchmaker's glass in his left eye and tinkered at something in the watch mechanisms with some microscopic graver. His work was interrupted only by mealtime or by the visit of a new customer. In accordance with camp etiquette the master received suitable remuneration for his efforts in the form of valuable provisions or cigarettes. In record time Lewin became persona grata to the entire camp, including the crew of esmen of higher and lower rank.

◆   ◆   ◆

The musical demands of Commander Schwarzhuber and his subordinates became ever greater and more importunate, to such an extent that in our present situation it was difficult to meet them. I suggested to Kopka that he get permission from the commander for two orchestra rehearsals a week to be held in the afternoon. I also had the faint hope that this would allow the musicians to take a slight breather after morning labor outside the camp.

Permission was given, the more willingly as the commander at the same time asked us to put together a potpourri, that is, a medley, from a few of the popular German operettas and also to orchestrate his favorite sentimental march, "Heimat, deine Sterne" (Fatherland, your stars). This march was the leitmotiv of a propaganda film, *Quax*, popular all over Germany. To hasten the completion of this "commission" the commander even allowed a temporary increase in the number of copyists, thanks to which a few newly arrived musicians were spared being sent to work outside the camp.

These two unheard-of favors given to "his" orchestra by the *Lagerführer* himself, the highest authority in the camp, were energetically opposed by . . . the prisoner Franz Danisch, who held the honorific position of *Lagerältester* (chief supervisor) of Birkenau. This Franz hated music, was our implacable enemy, and regarded the entire *Kapelle* as a bunch of freeloaders. And now the long-lasting silent conflict broke out into a heated debate between the *Häftling* (prisoner) Franz Danisch and the *Hauptsturmführer*, commander of Birkenau, Johann Schwarzhuber! And strangely enough, the latter did not always gain the upper hand and more than once had to postpone the completion of his favorite Fatherland and its stars. Danisch's arguments were irrefutable.

"I am responsible for completing the work on time, and for this I need hands and not some music copying or orchestra rehearsals!"

Danisch's origin was just as mixed as Kopka's: a half-Pole, half-German from Silesia. He was the real terror of Birkenau. Shortly after he arrived in the camp, he gained the confidence of the authorities with his denunciatory activities and was appointed chief of one of the most populous barracks. One day, on account of some serious breach of discipline, the Germans decided to give a severe flogging to all of the barracks chiefs without exception. When Danisch's turn came, he refused to bend over. On the contrary, he snapped to attention and addressed the esmen in the following words:

"How is this, you want to punish me? And for what reason? What happened was not the fault of the barracks chiefs. Solely to blame is the present *Lagerältester*, who is unequal to the task. Appoint me in his place and I promise you that similar incidents will never happen again and that Birkenau will become a model for other concentration camps!"

Though astonished by the audacity and tone of this speech, the Germans accepted Danisch's challenge. They did not flog him and without delay received from the commander his nomination to this position, the highest in the camp. Franz Danisch kept his word. In hardly more than a few days he achieved what his predecessor had been unable to do: replace camp discipline with terror.

I did not know Franz Nierychło, but those two Franzes, Danisch and Kopka, I will never forget. To perpetuate their memories in these pages is embarrassing to me.

◆   ◆   ◆

The rehearsals were inaugurated, however, and were held regularly twice a week. Apparently some compromise had been reached between Danisch and the *Lagerführer*. This did not prevent our caretaker from casting menacing but powerless glances at us from time to time.

The rehearsals were now taking place under my direction. This custom established itself spontaneously, as it were, because under various pretexts, fatigue or some important business to take care of in another barracks, Kopka kept handing the conductor's baton over to me. The truth of the matter was—I admit it without any scruples—that I had intentionally introduced into my orchestrations the greatest number of difficulties in rhythm, counterpoint, and syncopation, for the percussion instruments as well, which made it impossible for Kopka to conduct the rehearsals, let alone public performances! I have never regretted the use of this dirty trick.

These regular musical sessions, usually three hours long, gave me the opportunity to get better acquainted with the rest of the members of our group and to conclude that with respect to nourishment most of them were leading more or less the same miserable existence I was. Everyone tried as best he could somehow to improve his lot. This one sold soup for a portion of sausage; the other would exchange the soup for a piece of bread or maybe a cigarette. Being a mixture of various nationalities, the musicians communicated with each other in a colorful linguistic mishmash, accompanied by lively gesticulations.

A few of the musicians were a lot better off, especially the Dutchmen, most of whom were consummate artists, specialists in dance music and light music in general. The kapos and other dignitaries relished this kind of music and in the evenings would summon three or four musicians to their private *Stube* (room) for their own pleasure. This happened not only with Kopka's knowledge but with his official, hardly unselfish, consent: the musicians returned from their moonlighting loaded down with all sorts of goodies and cigarettes, a large part of which was appropriated by the *Kapellmeister.* So both sides profited from this arrangement.

Neither Lewin nor I took part in these evening expeditions; Lewin because he did not have to, I—because I was incapable of doing it.

My companion on the bed of boards was the flutist Menasche, a Greek, a certified physician from the University of Toulouse. Obviously, he spoke excellent French. All of us called him "doctor." A much younger countryman, Michael, an accordion player who had arrived at the same time, was his inseparable companion despite the considerable difference in ages. After evening roll call one could often see them rooted to the spot, arm in arm, just before the barbed wires. They would stare at the neighboring women's camp (the same one before which I had practiced my violin exercises), where the doctor's daughter and Michael's two sisters were. (Perhaps it was they who had called in my direction: *Brot! Brot!?*) Sometimes the two men succeeded in throwing a bit of food over to the other side. Other times they waited in vain for the appearance of their dear ones.

I do not know how Doctor Menasche managed to get hold of a dressing case of considerable dimensions containing quite a large amount of essential medical supplies like ointments of various kinds, pills, iodine, distilled water, gauze, aspirins, dressing materials, and creams. During work outside the camp, many a musician—or even a nonmusician from our barracks— suffered greater or lesser injuries that required immediate dressing. So the doctor did not lack for patients. In exchange for his services he received a small compensation from each patient, which in sum added up to a rather impressive "income," which he generously shared with his countryman. Both of them regularly put away a bit of food for the girls in the neighboring camp.

◆　　　　◆　　　　◆

Toward the end of 1943 the orchestra was transferred to Barracks 5, which was nearer the gate and the esmen's watchtower. This barracks was the home of the carpenters' detachment, the so-called *Zimmerei*, whose chief kapo (*Oberkapo*) was the popular and universally liked German Kurt Reinhold. His closest collaborators, assistants one might say, were two Poles: Kazimierz Andrysik, concentration camp number 89 (!), and Józef Papuga, number 12,049. On their initiative we were outfitted with a large room, a *Musikstube*, separated from the rest of the barracks, where there was also a place for two large tables, one for the copyists, another for Heinz Lewin and his watchmaking trade.

This close proximity of music and craftsmanship made our barracks a place of constant pilgrimages, not only by the better-off prisoners but also by the esmen, who often needed the services of the watchmaker or the carpenters' *Oberkapo*, not to mention the guests who visited us to listen to a bit of music. So the barracks was always in a stir and calmed down only during rehearsals.

Apart from this, at the orders of the commander—and strangely enough, with the consent of Danisch—outdoor concerts of light music were held every Sunday afternoon. These concerts enjoyed the attendance of prisoners and esmen. The continually expanding repertoire made possible a greater diversity of the programs.

It was said after the war that in the German concentration camps the hanging of runaway prisoners took place to the sounds of music. As far as Birkenau is concerned, I must categorically deny this. The orchestra took no part in such performances. I am not absolving the orchestra, I am absolving the Germans, who love music too much to use it for such prosaic purposes. To be sure, it did sometimes happen that we were playing on our podium when a column of doomed prisoners was marching on the other side of the barbed wire toward the gas chambers. But this was purely accidental, merely a coincidence.

I recall one of these Sunday afternoon concerts. We were playing, without much enthusiasm, the overture to some German operetta. The camp was strangely empty. From the watchtower the loud sounds of a radio reached us, which blended with our own music in a pleasant cacophony. This did not disturb our doctor-flutist, who at that moment was playing a sentimental and masterly solo on his instrument.

He played as though inspired, so absorbed in phrasing the showy melody that he did not perceive the long line of trucks packed with women, creeping toward the crematoria. With a smile, Doctor Menasche, proud of his performance, placed the instrument on his knees.

The trucks disappeared around the bend. In one of them was the doctor's daughter.

✦   ✦   ✦

My lot gradually improved. Two well-off Poles, Józef Waśko and Czesław Kluczny, were taking English lessons from me. (Thanks to them, I gained yet another pupil, also a Pole, who was to turn out to be my real savior, but I will talk about him later.) They paid me with bread, margarine, and potatoes, which I could now prepare for myself, thanks to Kopka's ever-more-frequent absences.

We thought that his jaunts had the sole aim of acquiring foodstuffs, but later it seemed that something quite unexpected and much more serious, even dangerous, was involved.

One afternoon on his return from one of these excursions, Kopka entered the barracks with an uneasy expression and announced to us that he would soon be released from the camp! In a body we all congratulated him on this unheard-of success, but our joy was so sincere and spontaneous that Kopka clearly became uncomfortable. He became embarrassed, and we did also. With fury he sailed into us,

"So, that's how it is! Your're thinking that you'll soon be rid of me! Not so fast, you'll have to wait a bit, for it's still a long time to my release!"

In fact, Kopka's release was no surprise to any of us. We had often wondered for what offense such a miserable creature had been put in the camp and whether it wasn't because of some error or misunderstanding. On the other hand, Kopka, despite being an official *Reichsdeutsch*, was of Polish-Czech origin and hence might have seemed suspect to the authorities. In any case, he was a pure-blooded Aryan, and in the present situation was suited for cannon fodder, whose shortage was now being painfully felt.

After Stalingrad more and more alarming news began to come from the eastern front—alarming for the Germans, of course. The ranks of the Hitlerite army were thinning, and ever-greater infusions of new blood were required. In all haste the authorities were liberating the "less dangerous" prisoners of German nationality to shore up the punch-drunk Wehrmacht. Hence Kopka's anger had two equally important sources: first, his release was linked with being sent to the front; second, he had to step down from the pedestal of being a well-off *Kapellmeister* to the status of an ordinary private, condemned in advance to hunger, cold, maybe even death.

Soon after this we learned, not without a certain disappointment, that Kopka's release would not take place for a month, after the required physical checkup. But since this checkup was linked with his transfer to the special *Quarantäneblock* (quarantine barracks), he would probably not be our frequent guest, and so there was nothing to worry about. Kopka also seemed satisfied, since he confided to one of his comrades: this month's delay is a big plus, for by that time the war might be over.

This made me the real, though unofficial, conductor of the orchestra, which now numbered forty musicians. I could work in peace and enrich the repertoire either on my own initiative or at the instructions of the commander and his subordinates. I could also conduct rehearsals and public performances as I liked, without the amateurish meddling of the titular *Kapellmeister*.

✦   ✦   ✦

My situation continued to improve, not only because of the position I had attained, but mainly because I had ceased to be scorned by all as a "millionaire." This was the name given by older prisoners with low numbers to newly arrived prisoners, who naturally got higher and higher numbers. We were now at number 130,000. And so my number, 49,543—a series from which very few were still alive—gave rise to universal respect. I was not eating so badly, had a finely shaved head, and had made for myself a new striped suit, a "fashionable" one, with bell-bottom trouser legs. The narrow-waisted jacket had a band on the left pocket with the artistically drawn figures of my number and the yellow and pink triangles making up the Star of David.

From Kopka I also inherited his last man Friday, a double bass player whose name was Grigori but whom everyone called George. He was a Russian prisoner, an honest boy who was devoted to me, a real "Russian soul." He cleaned my shoes, pressed my clothes, and above all prepared tasty, substantial meals for me whose leftovers fed him and a few other starving musicians.

One Sunday afternoon I was standing on the threshold of the barracks waiting for the musicians, who were forming up in the main lane before marching out for the traditional concert. At that moment Franz Kopka appeared in the distance and made his way in my direction. As he approached, his terrible appearance became more and more visible: emaciated, unshaven, somehow strangely shrunken and worn to a shadow, he looked to me like the image of misery and despair. I felt a little sorry for him, for I was aware that in comparison with him I looked as though I had stepped out of a men's fashion magazine.

Suddenly I heard the stentorian voice of Franz Danisch behind me, but this time it was addressed to Kopka. "Kopka, dear God, what a sight you are! If you don't know how you look, I'll tell you, like a makeshift *Kapellmeister!* Look at him," he continued, pointing at me, "that's how a real *Kapellmeister* should look. With him the orchestra sounds as it should! It's a real pleasure to watch the detachments going out to work!"

I could hardly believe my ears. Had Danisch finally declared peace on the orchestra and music in general? Everything seemed to say so.

After this, Kopka disappeared for a longer time; it was as though the ground had swallowed him up. We found out that he was being consumed by some mysterious illness and was bedridden. Almost every day he sent a messenger to me with an urgent appeal for food. After meeting his requests several times, I held a meeting with my colleagues, and we decided to stop sending these gifts and instead divide the surplus food among the more needy and deserving.

One day after another passed without incident. Everything seemed to indicate that we had gotten rid of Kopka once and for all. This was too good to be true.

Kopka appeared again like a ghost from the other world— and at the most inconvenient moment. The barracks was almost empty, everyone had gone out to work, and only the traditional foursome was sitting in the music room: Lewin, Weintraub, and I, and also George, who was bustling about the stove cooking up a meal for the four of us.

Kopka's intrusion put an end to this pleasant atmosphere. He was pale as a ghost, loathsome, breathing with hatred for the entire world and for me in particular. To give himself importance and authority he had decked himself out in his silver *Kapellmeister*'s lyre. He launched into a long tirade, interspersed with insults, none of which was understandable except one thing: that he wouldn't let me get away with it. In conclusion, a threat:

"So that's how it is? You think that you have gotten rid of me? That I'm finished? You're cooking up junkets for yourselves at my expense, eh? And nothing for me? I'll show you all!"

He went up to the stove, pushed George aside, and with an energetic motion of his arm dashed to the floor the pot with the cooking potatoes, the frying pan with the sausage, and the kettle of boiling water. We barely escaped being badly burned. But Kopka was still not satisfied. He ran up to Lewin's table and with the same motion of his outstretched arm swept off the watches, glasses, hands, precision instruments, everything he encountered in his way. Our beloved *Musikstube* looked like a battlefield. Was this the end? Would Kopka finally go? A vain hope. He turned to me, threatening me with his fist, and yelled,

"I'll tell everything to the *Lagerführer!* We'll go to him together, right now!"

I put on my jacket and followed Kopka in the direction of the watchtower. I was bathed in sweat. On the surface I was composed and put on as good a face as I could, but inside I was shaking with panicky fear. On the one side Franz Kopka, number from the 11,000 series, future soldier of the Wehrmacht; and I on the other, 49,000 series, a Jew with his Star of David. A too uneven contest, the outcome decided in advance. But I thought to myself: you only die once, a little sooner, a little later, what's the difference.

After waiting a quarter of an hour, we were standing before the commander.

"*Was ist los* (What's the matter)?"

Kopka pronounced his indictment.

"*Herr Hauptsturmführer*, this *Häftling* who is temporarily replacing me has made himself at home in the barracks, he cooks up private meals for himself from provisions that he gets from who knows where, probably stolen. That's not all, he composes and performs forbidden Polish music in the barracks . . ."

He did not get any further. The commander got up from behind his desk, walked up to Kopka, and gave him two slaps in the face. And now something completely unbelievable happened! *Lagerführer* Schwarzhuber tore off the band with the silver lyre from Kopka's arm and, looking him straight in the eye, shouted in anger,

"*Du Lump! Du Schwein! Raus!* (You wretch! You pig! Get out!)"

After which, turning to me, he handed me the shreds of the armband and said gently, almost kindly,

"*Und jetzt nenne Ich Sie Lagerkapellmeister* (and now I appoint you *Kapellmeister*)!"

For Kopka two slaps and addressed as "*du*"; for me the office of *Kapellmeister* and addressed politely as "*Sie*" . . . all-powerful music!

My colleagues were genuinely pleased and wished me all the best. A new silver lyre, embroidered at short notice, decorated my left arm. There was no news about Kopka after that. Later we learned that his illness had made galloping progress and that he had ended his miserable existence the day before his scheduled release.

And so instead of beefing up the ranks of the German army, his soul flew straight to the same *Himmelkommando* to which he had wanted prematurely to dispatch me.

◆   ◆   ◆

The "forbidden Polish music" for which Kopka had denounced me to the commander was not the sick invention of his vengeful mind. In fact, during one of his unexpected intrusions into the barracks he had caught us arranging a Polish piece, obviously in secret from the authorities. If some intruder had suddenly appeared, we were supposed immediately to start playing another piece that had been prepared in advance. I had not deemed this necessary in the presence of the now-harmless, or so I thought, Kopka, and so I had continued the rehearsal as though nothing had happened. A few words on the origin of this Polish music:

One evening a few weeks before the events described took place, on my way back from giving one of my English "classes," I found lying on the ground a crumpled and greasy piece of paper covered with writing that attracted my attention. I picked it up and, after returning to the barracks, unfolded it carefully so as not to tear it. It smelled of herring and God only knows what else. But it was music! Only the melody, written by hand but very legibly, without harmonization, without accompaniment. The title at the top read "Three Warsaw Polonaises of the 18th Century, author: Anonymous."

I washed the precious document as carefully as possible and hung it up in a discrete place in the music room to dry overnight. During the next few days I harmonized all three polonaises and wrote out the parts for a small chamber ensemble, after which we began to practice the pieces in the barracks when conditions allowed. The pieces turned out to be true pearls of eighteenth-century Polish music.[*]

Some of my Polish colleagues congratulated me on this deed, regarding it as an act of the resistance movement. This surprised me a little, since for me this was an ordinary musical satisfaction, heightened by the Polishness of the music to be sure, but I did not see how its being played in secret could have harmed the Germans or had an effect on the war. In any case, if

[*] After the war I recreated these three polonaises from memory. They were published in 1950 by the Polish Music Publishers in Kraków. (They appear in the Appendix of the present volume—ED.)

this episode can be regarded as a sign of resistance, it is the only one I can boast of during a rather long stay in Birkenau. The rest was a struggle for survival.

◆　　　　◆　　　　◆

After I returned to the barracks following the scene of Kopka's degradation and my promotion, our room had already been cleaned up. George was consuming the remnants of the salvaged tidbits while preparing a fresh meal for me. With his trusty watchmaker's glass in his eye, Lewin was as usual bent over his table sorting out hour and minute hands and other valuables that had been gathered up with difficulty from the mess on the floor.

And now an era of peace began. Everything seemed to indicate that nothing would disturb it for the time being. Except that with my position as titular *Kapellmeister* a new, sad duty was thrust upon me: to assign musicians for work outside the camp and to put them in this or that detachment depending on their musical qualifications. Taking advantage of Danisch's temporarily indulgent frame of mind, I wheedled out of him a privilege that no one before me had been able to gain: to send the musicians out on somewhat easier work, which would enable them to retain the nimbleness of their hands and fingers and thereby ensure a better sound and a more rhythmic cadence of the marches. On another occasion, when we were playing outside during a furious blizzard, I succeeded in convincing him to send us back to the barracks, and the rest of the detachments marched out without music. I obviously didn't use the argument that the musicians might take sick, for that would have been to no avail. On the other hand, what did convince him was the fear that the blizzard might damage the instruments. This became a precedent of sorts: the orchestra stopped going outside when bad weather threatened the instruments.

✦   ✦   ✦

A coincidence? A decree of propitious fate? The fact was that my situation—my food situation, that is—paradoxically improved with the advent of the new barracks chief, the horrendous Albert Haemmerle. There were many terrors in Birkenau, and every one of them seemed the greatest and the most menacing; but one can say without question that Albert Haemmerle had raised the art of dispassionate murder to the greatest heights.

He was one of the first inmates of the camp. He belonged to the "crew" of German *Häftlinge* who had been sent to Auschwitz with the mission of educating the first deported Poles in June 1940. He had been arrested as a common criminal and for this reason wore a green *Winkel* (triangle) on his chest. His sinister reputation had preceded him, and his arrival gave the entire barracks the cold shivers. We all knew that Haemmerle—like some other barracks chiefs on a smaller scale—did not sit down to his breakfast unless he had made mincemeat out of a dozen or more prisoners, especially Jews.

Albert Haemmerle was of less than average height, with a rather slender frame, and at first glance there was nothing that betrayed his tremendous physical strength. He had the reputation of being able to kill a man with one blow of his fist, especially when this man was a "Mussulman," a *Häftling* worn out with excessive labor and incapable of the slightest resistance. It turned out that the terrible havoc that Haemmerle spread in the barracks under his supervision finally alarmed the camp authorities. He was threatened with severe punishment if he did not restrain his murderous instincts. In other words, too much is not healthy. So we could expect that the form in which we inherited him would turn out to be somewhat milder than the previous version.

This dangerous neighbor and superior, who was usually enraged like a wild beast against everyone, this monster in human form, in record time became the friend and protector of the entire orchestra and of me in particular, in rather strange circumstances.

Albert Haemmerle was madly in love with a charming boy of exceptional beauty, a Pole—I'll call him Bolek—who acted as his "secretary" but lived in another barracks. Bolek had slightly effeminate features, perhaps too delicate, but hardly brazen; on the contrary, his face radiated irresistible, youthful charm, and I myself looked at him with great pleasure.

I had plenty of opportunities to see him: Bolek took English lessons from me, for he had heard about my linguistic and pedagogical skills. This put me on good terms with Haemmerle. Bolek knew German very poorly, and his "boss" obviously could not speak a word of Polish. So to some extent, when the need arose, I was the mediator between this pair that, for me, was heaven-sent. The relationship did not last long, but even its brevity turned out to be highly profitable.

One day a crushing blow fell on the invincible Haemmerle: without warning, like a bolt from the blue, the object of his passion dropped him for another camp VIP! The English lessons also went to blazes. Like a wounded animal, unmindful of the warning of the authorities, Haemmerle took out his fury on the innocent *Häftlinge*. The number of corpses beat all records.

The orchestra somehow did not suffer from this. On the contrary: the *Reichsdeutsch* spurned by a Pole sought forgetfulness in music. In free moments from his duties he had the musicians play sentimental melodies and romances, rewarding them with valued tidbits and drowning his sorrows with glasses of alcohol. After each musical seance, he invited me to his room to dictate to me passionate letters to Bolek in German which I later translated into Polish. As far as I know, the unfaithful Pole left these epistles unanswered; but each time I played the secretary, I emerged loaded down with generous gifts.

Soon after this Haemmerle disappeared from the horizon. He had supposedly been sent to the front. I became a little poorer, but the barracks sighed with relief.

◆   ◆   ◆

The following anecdote is popular all over the world among musicians and music lovers:

A certain foreign tourist, while crossing the main square of a German town, sees a rather sizable brass band playing before the balcony of the town hall. The tourist turns to one of the bystanders and asks,

"In whose honor is the band playing?"

"What do you mean, in whose honor? In honor of our mayor! Today is his birthday!"

"I understand. But why doesn't the celebrant show himself on the balcony?"

"Because he can't. He's playing in the band himself."

This anecdote pokes fun at the exaggerated love of the German nation for music. And there really is no doubt that the Germans are music lovers from birth and that nothing musical is alien to them. Their insistence on having music at a place like Auschwitz is only one example of this passion.

When an esman listened to music, especially of the kind he really liked, he somehow became strangely similar to a human being. His voice lost its typical harshness, he suddenly acquired an easy manner, and one could talk with him almost as one equal to another. Sometimes one got the impression that some melody stirred in him the memory of his dear ones, a girlfriend whom he had not seen for a long time, and then his eyes got misty with something that gave the illusion of human tears. At such moments the hope stirred in us that maybe everything was not lost after all. Could people who love music to this extent, people who can cry when they hear it, be at the same time capable of committing so many atrocities on the rest of humanity? There are realities in which one cannot believe. And yet . . .

◆   ◆   ◆

Commissions for new music poured down on me from all sides. The commander ordered the composition of two potpourris, one of them based on Schubert melodies, the other on Russian themes. The first was supposed to be called "Erinnerungen an Schubert" (Memories of Schubert). Lewin's help turned out to be very valuable in arranging this potpourri, since he knew the songs (there are more than six hundred of them!) of this composer better than I did. He also gave me some excellent ideas on what to start with, how to arrange the order of the melodies, and what to end with. The second potpourri had the title "Schwarze Augen" (Dark eyes, from the Russian song "Ochi Chorniye"). I had a fair knowledge of Russian themes but was an ignoramus in comparison with Weintraub, who could come up with an endless flow of Gypsy-Russian melodies. So with a common effort we worked up two fine instrumental fantasies that were warmly received by the esman audience.

One day *Blockführer* Stefan Baretzky (him I will remember!) brought us a march with the arrogant title "Deutsche Eichen" (German oaks), with an order, tinged with a threat, that we should play it whenever he, Baretzky, was within our sight, far away or close by, for otherwise . . .

Baretzky was no ordinary esman music lover. With respect to cruelty I would put him somewhere between Franz Danisch and Albert Haemmerle. Always crouched over astride his motorbike, he would race tirelessly from one end of the camp to the other, always appearing where he was least expected. In order not to incur his wrath we really should have done nothing else but continually play "German Oaks," to which his love for music was limited.

Another music lover, whose name I do not remember, brought me "Argonner Wald" (Argonne forest) and "Gruss an Obersalzberg" (Greetings to Obersalzberg), marches that he in turn was crazy about, and not without reason: first, this esman had fought in the murderous battle that raged in this forest in 1914–15; and second, he came from the vicinity of Obersalzberg, and so the second piece stirred in him tender childhood memories.

The commissions, of course, were "urgent," and so I had to work late into the night in order to finish the orchestration in time. Unfortunately, my effort turned out to be in vain, for we played both of these marches only halfway through in all. The commander had them both stopped in the middle: "Argonner Wald" because this battle, initially victorious for the Germans, ended in their overwhelming defeat in 1918. Better not to recall that. Obersalzberg, on the other hand, was one of the famous residences of the Führer, and it was unfitting for a camp orchestra consisting mostly of Jews to send him greetings there.

De gustibus non est disputandum. Unterscharführer Heinrich Bischop loved music . . . Jewish music. He would visit us on the sly, as it were, at unusual hours, and ask a few Dutchmen (they knew everything) to play, as quietly as possible, a few popular Jewish songs. We wondered where he got this taste from. Could he have been of "suspicious" origin? No, that was impossible! Perhaps it was simply some malicious perversion? In any case, a silent agreement was reached between Bischop and us. During his musical visits, we were careful not to be caught red-handed. One of our colleagues stood by the door to warn us of any sudden undesirable visit. The musicians played softly, not only to keep from being heard outside, but also because, when played quietly, Jewish melodies become more sentimental and moving. Bischop was in seventh heaven.

After the seances ended, our guest unvaryingly started looking for something in his pockets and, not finding anything, would borrow a pack of cigarettes from the watchmaker, distributing some of them to the performers and keeping the rest for himself.

These forbidden concerts did not last long. Apparently word about them reached the authorities, since one day Bischop vanished into thin air, not only from our barracks but from the camp itself. We learned some time later that, thanks to someone's denunciation, the authorities had found out about his sordid musical tastes and that straightaway he had been sent to the front.

◆　　　◆　　　◆

One of the most amusing clashes of music with camp discipline was unquestionably the episode with the "genre piece," a work intended for Sunday concerts. It was entitled "Die Postkutsche" or "The Mail Coach," and it had been commissioned by the *Lagerführer* himself. The piano score contained the instructions that "the solo trumpet at the beginning must sound as if it is coming from far away, pianissimo, and get louder as the mail coach approaches the town," for otherwise the work would completely lose its effect and the listener would not get the point.

I found myself at a loss: how could I get a similar effect from a trumpeter sitting motionlessly in the same place? And I had heard somewhere that the commander was very keen on hearing this effect. To have the trumpet play with a mute also made no sense, for whoever heard of a post horn played with a mute? To start with a mute and then take it out in the middle would also fail to give the desired effect. What to do?

Hierarchically and submissively I presented this "serious" problem to Franz Danisch. I explained to him as clearly as I could that for the "Mail Coach" to turn out according to the wishes of the *Lagerführer*, the trumpet soloist had to go outside the camp—far enough away that he would not be seen—and slowly make his way to our podium, where his solo was supposed to end with a triumphant trumpet call to the accompaniment of the entire orchestra.

Danisch scratched his head. This uncommon situation seemed to surpass his competency. After thinking for a long time, he made a difficult decision.

"We'll go together to the *Lagerführer*, and you will explain everything to him exactly. Maybe he will come up with something. If he wants to have a mail coach with a horn, let him rack his brains."

The *Lagerführer* listened to me attentively and found a solution on the spot.

"The soloist has to go outside the camp, that's obvious. But he will go under the supervision of a guard, who will walk behind him step-by-step until both of them return to the camp. This should give an excellent result."

And it did.

◆   ◆   ◆

Both potpourris, the one on Schubert and the Russian-Gypsy melodies, were enthusiastically received by the esmen. When we were playing the latter, the commander allegedly interrupted his work, stood by the window, and, lost in meditation, listened to the expansive music sung to him by the inscrutable Slavic soul.

One one memorable Sunday we were in the midst of performing this popular Russian fantasy. I was conducting the orchestra with a certain amount of enthusiasm, almost with inspiration, which was also passed on to the musicians, for they were playing better than ever before. In the corner of my eye I saw Baretzky standing by the gate. Legs astride his motorbike, hands on his hips, he stood with his head slightly cocked, as though defiantly. I paid no attention to him and conducted the concert to the end, convinced that he was listening to us like the others, with pleasure and approval.

I had hardly made the last wave of my baton when Baretzky suddenly rode up on his inseparable bike and told us to put our instruments away as quickly as possible, to assemble in full strength at the opposite end of the camp, and to wait for him there. It came to me in a flash. "Deutsche Eichen"! I had completely forgotten about it. We would not get away with this.

There was nothing for us to do but comply with his order and wait for the sentence.

After a few minutes Baretzky rode up, leaned his bike against a tree, and stood in front of our group. In his hands he held a thick, knotty stick. He gave a short speech, at first in a moderate tone, but he gathered strength and passion and finally ended with a shrill and completely unexpected command.

"There are various kinds of music in the world. For me there is only one: my music. And my music is 'Deutsche Eichen.' You all saw me standing by the gate and you calmly played on, as though I wasn't there, as though I didn't exist. You'll pay me for this, *brave Kerle* [fine fellows]! Jump to it! Squat! Get up! Squat! Get up! Kneel! Get up! Flat on your faces! Get up!"

Waving and belaboring us with his stick, Baretzky reeled off an endless litany of exercises at a dizzying pace. This was regarded as one of the severest physical punishments in the camp. It bore an innocent and noble name: sport. One had to be a pretty well-trained athlete to endure similar sport for more than five minutes, the minimum punishment. Those who were generally subjected to this punishment were weakened, under-nourished creatures incapable of great physical effort. Some of the musicians were in this condition, even though they were a little better-off than the rest of the prisoners.

The particular elements of that day's sport included squatting, getting up, running, leapfrogging, rolling on the ground, push-ups, running up and tumbling down hills, and other ingenious torments. One exercise followed another at a hellish pace, while our tormentor urged us on in a monotonous, icy voice. His stick did not pardon the least infraction, the least imperfection of execution. After a dozen or so seconds of this sport the sweat was running down us, we were panting, an unbearable pain was piercing our hearts, our ears were ringing, and we were close to fainting.

How much time had passed? A minute? Two, three? How many minutes of punishment had Baretzky decided to give us? Every second was an eternity. I looked at him from the corner of my eye. Was he just looking at the watch in his hand? Was this the end? No. Baretzky, unruffled, like an automaton, continued to reel off orders and shower blows.

We could hardly move, some of us had already fallen helplessly on the ground in a state of complete exhaustion. Another glance at his watch and Baretzky gave the sign to stop. He flung another threat at us in parting.

"This time I have satisfied myself with a lesser punishment: ten minutes. The next time I'll lay on a whole fifteen minutes. I wouldn't want to be in your shoes if it came to that."

Neither would we. Everything would depend on me, on my presence of mind. But I still didn't understand: when Baretzky appeared were we supposed to interrupt the music we were playing or were we to play it to the end and then start "German Oaks"?

The matter was cleared up in a few days. In the barracks we were rehearsing a popular Viennese waltz that had recently been brought to me, a song from a musical comedy at the Burgtheater.* A very pretty, sentimental melody, half song, half dance. We were playing very carefully, and all of us were really enjoying it.

Just as we were getting to the culminating point of the expressive mood, suddenly the eternal bane of our lives appeared on the threshold—Baretzky! With a brutal gesture I instantly interrupted the love theme and called out in a loud voice,

* A famous theater in Vienna.—ED.

"Deutsche Eichen"! But to my great astonishment Baretzky took exception with a kindly smile, *"Nein, nein, weiter machen,* continue playing."

And so the drawn-out theme was played to the end; there would be no punishment. I plucked up my courage, walked up to Baretzky, stood at attention, and asked submissively whether we were supposed to do this all the time: play the piece we had started to the end and then play his favorite march? The answer was *"Ja, ja! Weiter spielen, und dann— 'Deutsche Eichen'!"*

So at least I knew what I was supposed to do. The orchestra experienced no more sport on its own skin.

✦   ✦   ✦

Rapportführer Joachim Wolff was a frequent guest in our *Musikstube.* He had no special tastes, he liked all sorts of music, as long as it was not too loud. He was well mannered, and there was nothing "stiff" about him. He visited us like a neighbor. But we knew that the main reason for his visits was Heinz Lewin and unofficial chats with him. These were not private talks, however; they took place in my presence, and more than once I even took part in them.

Wolff gave the impression of being a mild man, incapable of the characteristic esman brutality. His watch was always in perfect condition, and unlike his comrades he did not come to Lewin as a watchmaker but for entirely different reasons. The source of his liking for Lewin was that both of them had seen the light of day in the same east German town of Halle-an-der-Saale. Every visit by Wolff was an additional link in the chain of friendship that seemed to link the German hangman with the non-German Jewish victim. After every one of Wolff's returns from leave, Heinz asked him for news about their common place of birth. Wolff willingly complied and talked about everything as if in a family circle. One time he described in great detail how much the town had suffered from enemy air raids, mentioning the streets, buildings, monuments, and relics that had literally been leveled to the ground.

These conversations usually took place late in the evening, when the camp was immersed in an ominous silence, interrupted by occasional rifle shots in the distance.

One evening Heinz asked Wolff a delicate question that had been troubling us for a long time. The shots were resounding more frequently than usual, and the time seemed ripe for unburdening ourselves.

The German army was retreating all along the eastern front. A state of emergency had been announced throughout the Reich. Any month or even any week the landing of the Allied forces was expected on the northern coast of France. The whole camp knew about this, the news had passed through the grapevine. Heinz Lewin's curiosity seemed entirely natural to Wolff.

"*Herr Unterscharführer,* do you think the Germans can still win the war?"

"Not necessarily," Wolff answered after reflecting briefly, "the chance is less and less."

"If that's so, then after all . . . everything that is going on here . . . here and in other camps . . . the world will find out about it, if it doesn't know already. Don't you think that the Germans will have to pay the piper?"

"Not at all. There will be no account to settle. No one will find out about anything."

"I understand . . . you want to say that none of us prisoners will get out of here alive, that there will be no eyewitnesses . . ."

"By no means! That's not what I wanted to say . . ."

A long silence. Wolff seemed to be gathering his thoughts together, weighing the words that would best express them. He began to speak slowly, as though he were doing something forbidden.

"You see, perhaps it's even better for you to know how things really stand. In fact, according to the instructions of the Führer himself, not even one *Häftling* should come out alive from any concentration camp. In other words, there will be no one who can tell the world what has happened here in the last few years. But even if such witnesses should be found—and this is the essence of the brilliant plan of our Führer—NOBODY WILL BELIEVE THEM. It was he who began and put into practice something exceptionally simple, but which surpasses the power of comprehension of the non-German civilized person. I understand, to all of you this seems 'monstrous,' 'incomprehensible,' 'barbaric,' but only because you belong to a different race. Even if we lose the war, which is not yet certain, no one will present us with the reckoning. At most a few bigwigs will have to bear the consequences. Your 'judgment,' if it ever comes to that, will have to take place in a court, which will base itself on antiquated legal formulas that have no application to our 'crimes.' Your judges will be forced to declare their own incompetency, since no human court can punish lawlessness with lawlessness. The Germans will come out of this unscathed and will live forever."

❖　　　❖　　　❖

Rottenführer Pery Broad was probably our most frequent guest and the most faithful friend of our orchestra. A strange, colorful, and disturbing phenomenon, in a certain sense he was a prodigy. He was not quite twenty-two years old, a twerp one might say, yet he had already risen to the position of chief of the Political Bureau (*Politische Abteilung*) at Birkenau. He was born in Rio de Janeiro of a Brazilian father and a German mother. Mixed marriages supposedly give excellent results, and Pery Broad was an exemplary confirmation of this theory. It was he who decided the fates not only of individual *Häftlinge* but also, and for the most part, of entire national groups. "Decided the fates" meant death in the gas chambers. Pery Broad owed this honored function primarily to his nearsightedness, which exempted him from active service and allowed him to follow the voice of his calling.

During the trial held in Frankfurt am Main after the war, there was a lot of talk about the numerous crimes committed by this whippersnapper. As far as I know, though, no one mentioned his uncommon musical talents, not as a way of bringing in mitigating circumstances but simply as an example of a rarely encountered association—is it typically Teutonic?—of unbridled criminality and the heights of artistry.

Pery Broad gave the impression of being an intellectual of the first water, an impression emphasized by his glasses, which never left his nose. He was fluent in several languages, and nothing in his behavior or manner suggested his trade. He would appear in our music room with a carefree expression, smiling, like a friend from the university, or rather from the conservatory.

Broad's instrument was the common, vulgar accordion. I had always had contempt for this popular contraption, which I regarded as a certain kind of musical bastard suited only for playing on the streets and begging. And here in the person of Broad I met a genuine artist, a virtuoso of the highest class, in both group and solo performances. Under his long, aristocratic fingers, nimbly darting over the keys and registers, with the simultaneous moving of the bellows back and forth, the accordion I had held in contempt was instantly rehabilitated into the great family of musical instruments.

Broad was primarily a lover of jazz. He knew by heart almost all the American and European hits. Unlike Bischop, he made no secret of his visits or of his musical exhibitions. He most often played with a few of our best virtuosos, a violinist, clarinetist, trumpet player, trombonist, and a percussionist—all Dutchmen, of course. But sometimes he got the urge to put on a solo display. He would then improvise breakneck runs, dizzying passages, and chords and rhythms combined with such dash that more than one serious composer would have envied him.

Sometimes a scowl of impatience would distort the delicate features of the artist. He would then throw down the accordion in anger and swear through his teeth, *verfluchtes Zeug* (damned piece of junk)! Indeed, our four accordions, continually exposed to bad weather, had been in a sorry state for some time, and it was no wonder that an artist of his stature was not content with them. So one afternoon Broad brought his own instrument. It was a real beauty, a brand-new accordion equipped with all the latest improvements, numerous basses and as many chords. Only then did we become aware of what heights the mastery of this artist could reach when he found himself in his element, that is, when he played on an instrument with which he was familiar.

But even this exquisite accordion did not entirely satisfy its owner. Broad's dream was to equip it with an additional register, namely, one that would imitate the sound of a French horn with a mute. Obviously, Heinz Lewin was the only one to undertake such a task, and at the cost of long days of tinkering in the insides of the instrument he completed this difficult job faultlessly. Broad was beside himself with joy, and he offered a suitable remuneration: Heinz received 250 cigarettes, a king's ransom!

There were periods when Broad's visits were irregular. We knew then that he was occupied with entirely different matters, which absorbed him no less than music did. Not long before, he had been saddled with the mission of recruiting a certain number of women prisoners for a brothel the authorities had established in Auschwitz I, to be frequented by esmen and camp VIPs alike. The latter were conducted there from Birkenau under proper escort, which subsequently brought them back.

Recently Broad had disappeared from our horizon for much longer than previously. It concerned a trifle: the burning of a few thousand Gypsies and then the same number of Czechs. These holocausts took place "in secret" before the prisoners: the order was then issued for a *Blocksperre* (closing of the barracks), during which time the prisoners were forbidden to stick their noses over the threshold. On account of this "secrecy," however, everyone knew what was going on, not to mention that for long days the oppressive odor of burnt human flesh had been blowing in from the crematoria.

So is it any wonder that after performing such deeds Broad longed for relaxation among us musicians, to the sounds of his favorite accordion enriched with a new register?

❖   ❖   ❖

Lagerführer Hauptsturmführer Schwarzhuber never visited our barracks personally, or any other for that matter. He used to send all of the musical instructions to the orchestra either through a messenger or through one of the *Blockführer*. And here suddenly a strange exception: Franz Danisch in the flesh, out of breath, sweating, burst into the barracks like a bolt of lightning and in a choking voice announced to me that the commander's birthday was in three days, on Sunday, and that on this occasion he would visit the camp with his family. I had to compose a festive bugle call to greet them. The orchestra would take up its position on the podium long before the arrival of the distinguished family. This urgent commission was accompanied by no petty favor: for the few days that remained before the celebration the musicians would be exempt from going out to work in order to practice as much as necessary and to prepare themselves properly for the Sunday concert.

I did not believe that the bugle call idea had been hatched in Danisch's upper story; rather, I was inclined to believe that the *Lagerführer* himself had saddled Danisch with this honorific mission, simultaneously convincing him that it was his own (Danisch's) idea. In any case, these three days off from hard labor were filled with feverish work on the bugle call and the entire Sunday program.

But the best-laid plans . . . Like military strategy, the fixed plan of exterminating a fragment of humanity took no account of birthdays or festivities celebrated by private individuals, no matter how highly placed.

Blind chance had it that this Sunday family holiday of *Hauptsturmführer* Schwarzhuber's coincided—like an arranged meeting—with the procession of a crowd of thousands walking submissively toward the gas chambers. We had long since become accustomed to this sight. From our podium we could clearly see the undulating column of the doomed, surrounded on both sides by closely placed esmen armed to the teeth. Enticed by the sounds of music, they turned their heads in our direction. Perhaps they thought that since there was music, things would not be so bad for them.

Franz Danisch was clearly surprised by this unexpected intrusion. There had obviously been some error in the timetable; this transport had not been expected until tomorrow. Danisch kept watching for the commander's car that was scheduled to arrive at any moment, running back and forth like a madman from the gate to the stage. The orchestra was playing some overture; I was making mechanical gestures with my baton. . .

Then at a sign from Danisch the crowd became motionless, as though spellbound. The commander's car drove up and stopped near the gate. At the same time, the triumphant bugle call of four trumpets pierced the air. Schwarzhuber's elegant figure emerged from the car. He stood at attention and saluted, raising his hand to the visor of his cap. Danisch, stiff, with chest thrown out and bared head, stood rooted to the ground nearby, ready to run up at a nod from the commander.

The rodomontade bugle call came to an end. We began the first number of the program, obviously "Heimat, deine Sterne." The commander helped three persons get out of the car, his wife and two children, about six and eight years old. The woman, exhibiting beauty and freshness, stood beside her husband and tenderly leaned against his arm. On both sides of the charming couple stood the children, two cherubs. The commander whispered something into his wife's ear, pointing to the camp and the crowd of victims waiting motionlessly. He probably told her that the enemies of the Führer and the Third Reich were being punished. But he certainly did not tell her everything.

✦   ✦   ✦

"The Germans will come out of this unscathed and will live forever." These words of *Rapportführer* Joachim Wolff haunted me like the Evil One, in whom no one believes but who mercilessly besets us from all sides. It was now plain that Hitler's war plans conceived on a massive scale ran on several independent tracks, each of which had been laid out by a different hand, with one hand having no idea what the others were doing. News was coming in from the fronts (a secret eavesdropping device was supposedly operating in the camp) portending the inevitable, imminent defeat of Germany. But how could one believe this, when before our eyes moved innumerable crowds of people brought here from all corners of conquered Europe? Russians, Poles, Frenchmen, Dutchmen, Hungarians, Czechs, Greeks, Gypsies, Bulgarians—Jews and non-Jews—a veritable modern Tower of Babel. Lured by our sirenic music, this swarm moved ceaselessly to its place of execution.

In the memoirs of one of the generals of the Wehrmacht— I have forgotten his name—the author sets forth the thesis that one of the main reasons for Germany's defeat was the shortage of rolling stock for the transportation of troops and supplies. Individual commands called for reinforcements, but Hitler was implacable: priority went to the transportation of Jews to the extermination camps; the aim was to finish off everybody before the end—no matter what kind of end—of the war. It is hard to believe. But is it important whether one believes it or not? Who can deny that Hitler was more successful with the Jews than with the war?

In his memoirs entitled *Inside the Third Reich*, Albert Speer tells how, after leaving to its fate the 200,000-man Sixth Army (some sources say 250,000) encircled in the Stalingrad "cauldron," Göring "invited us to a festive performance of Wagner's *Die Meistersinger von Nürnberg* in the newly rebuilt Berlin Opera that had been destroyed by bombs in 1941. Decked out in ceremonial uniforms and dress coats, we took our places in the Führer's huge box. The carefree mood that prevailed there created such a painful contrast to what was going on at the front that for a long time I reproached myself for accepting this invitation."

In another place Speer wrote (I give this in abridgment): "After the symphony concert that was held in Berlin in the middle of December 1944 under the direction of Wilhelm Furtwängler, the latter asked me point-blank whether the Germans still had some chance of winning the war. I said no and knowing that on account of some of his sincere public statements Furtwängler might be exposed to repressions on the part of the Allies, I advised him not to return to Germany after his scheduled festival in Switzerland. Furtwängler protested, 'And what will happen to my orchestra? After all, I am responsible for it!' I promised him that I would personally attend to his musicians. I had not foreseen that Goebbels would stop me from doing this. For he had decided that the musicians, like everyone else, would take an active part in the defense of Berlin: 'This orchestra owes its high level and the recognition it enjoys in the world exclusively to me and my subsidies. Those who remain after us do not have the right to it! It can die along with us!' "

There is no rule without an exception. Goebbels was remarkably unmusical.

◆   ◆   ◆

They say that one can get used to anything, to the worst, to the most monstrous things. But I have never been able to fathom the mystery of the typical camp phenomenon that cannot be

called anything else but *habituation*. Habituation to everything that is going on around us and of which we naturally become indifferent witnesses. Habituation to a sea of human
beings scurrying off passively into the abyss of the crematoria,
habituation to the stink of bodies breathed day and night, habituation to the chaotic jumble of hunger and overeating, extreme
poverty and the prosperity that feeds on it, horror and hopeful-
ness.

After a sufficiently long stay in the camp, the monotony of
the hell in which we lived became thoughtless, unconcerned,
trivial everyday reality. Good news from the front, indicating
the defeat of Germany and the end of the war, was of no concern to us. It did not concern us because our own end would
come first. For every one of us such news came from a world we
had known a long time ago, a world that for us was a distant,
dead and buried world. We all had only one thought: why not
take advantage of the last moments of life since everything else
already belongs to the land of dreams?

Everyday we stood eye to eye with a ghastly two-sided coin:
on the one side—hell; on the other—the benefits this hell con-
ferred on Fortune's darlings, namely, on those who had become
"habituated."

The sea of people that the cattle cars from all over Europe
disgorged day in and day out left behind on the platform tower-
ing heaps of valises, suitcases, bags, parcels, and bundles filled
with food, tidbits, alcohol, jewels, money, gold coins, and various kinds of precious objects—all of which their owners would
never see again. These treasures fed the camp, both its residents (not all of them, obviously) and our esmen caretakers,
though in principle these things were to be sent to the heart of
the Reich to shore up the tottering economy.

There was a separate detachment in the camp for segregating and transporting these Jewish treasures. It was officially called the *Aufräumungskommando* (cleaning-up detachment), but its members gave it the slang expression "Canada"—symbol of abundance and plenty—a name that was quickly accepted among the *Häftlinge* and in the official terminology of the administration.

"Canada" initially numbered two hundred persons, but even when it reached eight hundred it could hardly keep up with servicing the splendidly equipped newcomers. The esmen supposedly kept a strict watch over the bustling "Canadians," but they overlooked petty and less than petty thefts, which the latter committed almost ostentatiously, for it was no secret to anyone that a considerable part of the booty would remain in their hands. The Canadians were subjected to a symbolic, very superficial search after their return to the camp, but this had been anticipated: master tailors had fitted their jackets and trousers with deep pockets and hiding places that could hold no mean treasures, especially as far as small things were concerned.

An uninterrupted stream of all kinds of precious objects flowed into the camp: jewels, cigarettes, chocolates, watches, spirits, perfumes, elegant underwear, cans of preserved vegetables, fruits, and meat. And all of this took place under the intentionally distracted eyes of the esmen of higher and lower rank, who would also benefit from the generosity of . . . the prisoners.

These manipulations, conducted on a massive scale, gradually formed the economic and social world inside the camp, with its privileged and oppressed groups, "domestic" and "foreign" trade, and market prices and their fluctuations. We even had our own currency, whose value no one questioned: the cigarette. The price of every article was stated in cigarettes. In cases of greater influx there was a surplus, and everything became proportionally cheaper. When the lack of "fuel" was felt, there was an unavoidable rise in prices, and some "tradesmen" resorted to prices expressed in halves or even quarters of cigarettes. Butts were also in demand and had their price. In "normal" times, that is, when the candidates to the gas chambers were coming in at a regular pace, a loaf of bread cost twelve cigarettes, a three-hundred-gram package of margarine, thirty; a watch, eighty to two hundred; a liter of alcohol, four hundred cigarettes!

After the fashion of independent countries, we also conducted trade overseas. Our overseas market was the civilian workers and technicians assigned by camp authorities to the various camp detachments, with which they were in constant contact. They were big consumers of various articles and commodities, including clothing, underwear, shoes, and, obviously, food—treasures that only the prisoners of Birkenau were able to provide. In the ranks of the detachments that marched out every morning to work there were many who wore almost new clothes or underwear under their regulation stripes and shoes in excellent condition; others had in their pockets precious stones or foreign currency. All of this would pass into the hands of the civilians, in exchange for which the same pockets on return to the camp would be filled with butter, vodka, meat, fowl, and various other tidbits.

All of this trading, supposedly secret but in reality recognized and tolerated, even supported by the authorities, had its commonly accepted name, though no one knew who had invented it. To engage in this activity was to *organize.*

To *organize* or to *organize for oneself* meant to acquire some object by any means at all. It could be through purchase (for cigarettes), begging, theft, swindling, violence, murder.

One *organized* a piece of bread or ten loaves of bread; a miserable, verminous rag or new silk underwear; one cigarette or a thousand cigarettes; a liter of soup or a kettle of soup; a sliver of wood, a board, ten boards, a table or . . . an entire barracks. One *organized* a pinch of salt, a bucket of coal, a straw mattress, medicine, a bed of boards—everything the heart desired if there were means for it and a bit of typical camp savvy.

Our cozy music room was organized from top to bottom with the consent of Kurt Reinhold, the *Oberkapo* of the carpenters' detachment, our roommates. To be sure, the camp authorities had given us permission for the planned improvements, but they had not shown the least interest in the means at our disposal for realizing them. They advised us as usual, "Organize this yourselves." How, from where, with whose help, was of no concern to anyone.

After not very long negotiations we made a deal with Kurt Reinhold: the carpenters' detachment would supply us with materials and labor in exchange for lessons on the accordion for Reinhold's foreman and subordinate, Józef Papuga, under the condition that Papuga would also be able to practice in our room. In camp lingo this boiled down to the formula: the orchestra organized itself a music room and Józef Papuga organized himself lessons on the accordion. Both sides made a good deal.

Another example, tragic even in the camp but also typical of the mentality that had taken root in our world:

For a while a "Czech camp" that had come from Theresienstadt (Terezín) had existed near us. The *modus vivendi* of these Czech Jews was envious. They lived together with their wives and children, retained their long hair and ancient hairstyle, did not go out to work, and were pretty well-fed. They had their own musical group of more than a dozen members. In short, a paradise against the background of the nearby hell, but there was something ominous about it. Then one fine day the terrible news . . . The impression it made on us proved that we had still not become completely insensitive. It began very innocently.

Our music stands, which had long since become rotted from continual exposure to the elements, could barely stand up straight and were hardly fit for use. The carpenters had promised us to fix some of them and to put together a few new ones, but somehow they seemed in no hurry to do so. I had whispered a word to Danisch about this matter.

After a few days a messenger came with instructions for us to report immediately to the commander with a few musicians but without instruments. We went there, highly intrigued.

After the regulation "Attention! At ease!" the commander pointed to twelve black music stands in the corner and told us to take them, explaining: "I heard that you need music stands. Take these. I organized them especially for your orchestra."

We recognized those stands. They came from the Czech camp, which we had once had the opportunity of visiting on official business. Last night the four thousand Czechs, whom we had envied for their carefree prosperity, had been turned into ashes. That was the price of these music stands.

Along with the stands we also inherited from the Czechs a few violins, a trumpet, and a priceless violoncello, whose lack I had painfully felt. Not only would it enrich the sound of our orchestra, but it would give me the opportunity of forming a string quartet, writing from memory a few works of the great masters and also composing my own work for this classical group.

◆   ◆   ◆

Like everywhere in the world, we had our small, average, and big organizers. After evening roll call and before lights-out, small groups of striped prisoners would gather in the most secluded corners of the camp to organize whatever they could. They scattered like lightning at the sight of an approaching uniform.

However, there were more isolated and much safer places for all kinds of transactions, places from which potential traders would not be scared away. One such place was a huge latrine at the end of the camp in a barracks that from the outside looked like the others and that could accommodate up to six hundred persons at a time. Deals of all sorts were made there; one could exchange anything for something. The camp latrine was the marketplace of the dregs, a bazaar, a flea market, the hangout of the *Lumpenproletariat.*

A small room separated from the rest of the latrine by a solid partition was reserved for the camp VIPs, kapos, barracks chiefs, clerks, warehousemen, and so forth. An ordinary mortal would not dare cross the threshold of this preserve. There are various kinds of apartheid.

Transactions of an entirely different kind took place in the private rooms of the camp aristocrats, not only with the approval of the esmen but often with their secret participation. Trading went on there in watches, diamonds, dollars and other currencies, vodka, and of course food on a wholesale scale. There one could also plan an escape of one or a few *Häftlinge* outfitted in German uniforms. This was an organized escape in the double sense of the word.

All records in organizing were topped by the irreplaceable Kurt Reinhold, the favorite of both prisoners and esmen of higher and lower rank. He was a man of irresistible charm, who radiated a genuine goodness that was accompanied by rarely encountered generosity. To be sure, as we will see in a moment, he could afford it.

Reinhold had wandered from camp to camp for nearly ten years. It was said that he had been arrested for serious tax violations and thus had worn a green triangle on his pocket for a long time. Recently the authorities had relieved him of this dubious distinction and had absolved him of wearing any identification signs at all. This was supposed to be a reward for his "exceptional" services. What kind, no one knew. This privilege was accompanied by still another: the right to let his hair grow. Reinhold joked that he could not take advantage of this favor, since he was completely bald.

Kurt Reinhold really led the life of Riley, for which in those days more than one Croesus at liberty would have envied him. His breakfast consisted of two eggs, butter, ham, jam, real coffee, and no less real milk. He also had an impressive stock of all sorts of German and foreign wines, liqueurs, and spirits. The esmen deemed it an honor to be invited to his table. At the construction site outside the camp, where Reinhold went everyday at the head of his detachment, he had constructed with his "own" means a comfortable shed that protected him from the elements and that was a place of pilgrimage for chance guests, civilians and military men.

The construction and business activities Reinhold conducted on a hard-to-imagine scale could be the subject of a separate booklet of no mean size. The camp authorities had entrusted him with all the materials supposedly allocated to the construction of the camp barracks. Reinhold disposed of these materials as he saw fit and did not have to make an account to anyone, although in theory he was supposed to submit a report every three months on the materials used and the work completed.

Eight hundred persons were too many for one *Oberkapo* to look after. So Reinhold picked several trusted collaborators, both in the area of real construction work and, mainly, in the field of the notorious organization. It was the latter who were entrusted with the mission of exchanging construction materials for other valuable articles on the black market. Through them *Oberkapo* Reinhold supplied the privileged *Häftlinge* with building materials and everything else necessary for organizing themselves private rooms isolated from the rest of the barracks.

Kurt Reinhold's most numerous and most faithful customers, however, were the esmen themselves, starting from the commander and ending with the lower ranks. In addition to the elegant cottages that were springing up near the camp like mushrooms after a rain, twenty expert carpenters under his supervision made luxurious furniture. All of this went on almost in the open, under the open sky, to the irretrievable harm of the plan for expanding the Auschwitz camps and subcamps.

Was this why such masses of newly arrived deportees were sent straight to the crematoria?

◆   ◆   ◆

Music is an article of consumption par excellence and as such was subject to the skill of organizing. This had already been done in Kopka's time on a small scale. Now, with the continually increasing influx of "gas meat" and the accompanying prosperity of the privileged classes of Auschwitz society, this industry took on the dimensions of hitherto unknown luxury.

Almost everyday I was visited by some camp bigwig who asked me to lend him a few musicians, since he wanted to celebrate his name day, birthday, or some other family holiday properly. I willingly agreed. This was in the musicians' interest and mine as well, for the request was always backed by some gift that I could not afford to refuse.

In accordance with the fixed custom, the celebration took place in two stages:

The first took place at dawn. The musicians chosen, generally three or four, got up from their pallets earlier than the others so that they could awaken the celebrant before reveille with the sounds of a triumphant march or serenade. The hero of the festivities would pretend convincingly that this attention was a complete surprise to him and moved him deeply. He would quickly get up and hand the musician–alarm clocks various presents. This introductory ceremonial ended with a sentimental romantic tune and traditional greetings, which the musicians had learned in several languages, for sometimes there were non-German celebrants.

The second act of the holiday most often took place in the VIP's private room, after evening roll call and with the participation of a larger number of musicians. The guests would sit down to an amply set table, with plenty of food and drink. After the meal, the company, quite tipsy and moved to tears, would recall their remote, precamp days, all the while crooning melancholy songs or frivolous airs—German obviously. It sometimes happened that some esman unexpectedly barged into this sanctuary of camp bliss, to get a bite to eat and to down a glass of schnapps. This in no way disturbed the prevailing atmosphere; the merrymaking continued and sometimes lasted late into the night.

These evenings could not compare, however, with the celebration of the birthday of *Oberkapo* Kurt Reinhold, an event long remembered by the camp inmates. After a "sweet" awakening, Reinhold got up from his bed in his silk pajamas and from his personal cabinet took out a few hundred cigarettes and a few bottles of liqueurs, which he distributed not just to those who had roused him from his slumbers but to the entire orchestra. When half an hour later he was marching out to work at the head of his detachment, we interrupted the march we were playing with a triumphant bugle call in his honor. In the evening was held the banquet that Reinhold had previously organized in his own honor and to which he invited not only companions from the camp but also a few esmen officers. Spirits, wines, beer, champagne, flowed in streams. In the atmosphere of the general drinking bout Reinhold good-naturedly admitted to all present that in the last six months—with the consent of the authorities—he had managed to squander enough timber and other materials of various kinds to build thirty-five barracks!

This revelation greatly amused the entire company, and in order to celebrate this marvelous deed they all drank to Reinhold's health, and to the *Lagerführer*'s, and ended the celebration with the shout "Heil Hitler!"

✦   ✦   ✦

Keeping pace with these carefree libations, the rate of influx of human fuel did not slacken for an instant. One would not have been possible without the other. The Canada crew was unable to cope with the task. It was beefed up with recruits from less encumbered detachments, but even that was not enough. So my musicians were also harnessed to this lucrative work. I was left in peace, since the writing of music was no less important. Was I disappointed then by this distinction? I cannot answer that question.

My musicians returned delighted from these expeditions,

loaded down with food, drinks, valuables, and other organized precious things. I was also satisfied: a well-fed musician plays better than a hungry one.

The fruitful cooperation of the orchestra with the Canadians lasted a few weeks, during which time the musicians, and I along with them, ate as never before. No one thought about where the gifts consumed with relish had come from, no one was brushed by the slightest qualms of conscience, no one had any scruples. Everyone had only one thought: to fill his stomach, to regain the lost calories, to get rid of the look of a Mussulman, to survive at all cost.

After the Canadian adventure, they sent us—this time I went as well—to the storage camp (*Effektenlager*), not to play music, but to bring over disinfected clothing, underwear, shoes, and other things that had been stripped from the Jewish victims before they were gassed. These items were obviously destined for shipment to Germany.

Like others, this small camp was surrounded by a network of barbed wire. Inside was a double row of barracks like ours, but they were filled with things instead of human beings. Pieces of clothing were arranged in one; in the second, underwear; in the third, shoes; in the fourth, valises, and so on; everything separated in ideal order. In one corner of the camp we saw something like a rubbish heap, in which one could distinguish spectacles, books, prayer books, dolls, photographs, canes, umbrellas, pocketbooks, purses thrown in disarray . . . What the purpose of this junk pile was it was difficult to guess. Who could have foreseen that one day it would be shown on the screen as an exhibit of Nazi crimes and that some of us would see it?

This vast amount of stored and carefully inventoried treasures was taken care of by women prisoners who never went outside the barbed wire. They were young, attractive, elegantly dressed women—not in stripes—they looked like ladies from café society. The only things that identified them as prisoners were the camp number and triangle fastened to their chests.

Obviously, everything these women consumed and everything they wore came from the organization tolerated by the authorities. They had continual contact with both basic commodities and articles of luxury. Is it any wonder that a gulf separated them from their sisters in captivity vegetating in the depths of poverty and despair hardly a few hundred meters from here? These charming creatures lived in snug, comfortably furnished rooms with windows, curtains, shutters, and everything else required to feel at home. They slept in primitive but comfortable beds, with fluffy quilts and regularly changed bed linen. They had all sorts of cosmetics, perfumes, silk stockings, and beautiful hair styles as though they had just emerged from the hands of the most expert hairdresser. Except for freedom they had everything one could wish. The surroundings and the frequent visits by men, *Häftlinge* and esmen, were conducive to intimate trysts stolen from everyday life. In short—paradise behind barbed wire.

◆   ◆   ◆

On Christmas eve of 1943 I took a small group of Dutchmen to the women's hospital, where at the instructions of Commander Schwarzhuber we were supposed to play a few carols to console the sick. In addition to the "Three Warsaw Polonaises," I had once orchestrated several German and Polish carols, pieces highly suitable for this occasion.

I would rather not describe the sight that spread out before our eyes or the stink that blew on us when we crossed the threshold. It was unbelievable that this was a hospital whose calling was the treatment and care of weak, emaciated women who were near death. I chased away gloomy thoughts. We had come here to play, not to lament over the fate of others. So we played, hardly able to breathe.

We started with the traditional German carol "Silent Night, Holy Night" (among the sick were a few German women, the rest were almost all Polish), which the audience listened to attentively. In our repertoire we still had "Sleep, Little Jesus," "He Lies in the Cradle," "They Came Running to Bethlehem," and "God Is Born." We began with the first. After a few bars quiet weeping began to be heard from all sides, which became louder and louder as we played and finally burst out in general uncontrolled sobbing that completely drowned out the celestial chords of the carol.

I didn't know what to do; the musicians looked at me in embarrassment. To play on? Louder? Fortunately, the audience itself came to my rescue. From all sides spasmodic cries, ever more numerous, ever shriller—in Polish, which I alone understood—began to roll in on me: "Enough of this! Stop! Begone! Clear out! Let us croak in peace!"

I got the impression that if these creatures had not been so weakened, they would have flung themselves on us and pummeled us with their fists.

What could we do? We cleared out.

I did not know that a carol could give so much pain.

◆   ◆   ◆

Before they went to the gas chamber the Gypsies had enjoyed considerable privileges. Among other things, they had their own well-stocked canteen. After they were gone, something had to be done with it. The authorities decided to move it to the women's camp and once more saddled my musicians with this chore. By now camp discipline had visibly slackened, even become remiss, and my subordinates took advantage of this situation to drag out these excursions as long as possible.

This time close friendships were made, and nearly everyone had a more-or-less advanced flirtation going on there. If Doctor Menasche's daughter had been alive, I could have seen her almost every day, sometimes even a few times a day. On the other hand, his friend Michael always went along with his colleagues: both of his sisters were members of . . . the women's camp orchestra.

It had been established much later than ours, but its main task was the same: to provide rhythm for the women's detachments marching in and out. In this respect, there were completely equal rights in the Hitlerite concentration camps. The embryo of this group had been a bass drum and double cymbals. Gradually new instruments were added, mainly mandolins, guitars, a few violins, a violoncello, a few singers, even a grand piano(!), whose lack I had so painfully felt at the beginning of my career as an arranger when I had to harmonize and orchestrate by memory the melodies that were supplied to me.

The specific composition of the women's orchestra gave it a mild, sentimental quality, lacking the robustness that ours had thanks to the wind instruments, especially the brass. So most of the musicians, including me, held this "effeminate" music in contempt, which did not prevent a serious and loyal musical rivalry from developing in the commands of the two camps. Each of them praised the merits of "its" *Lagerkapelle* to the skies. A certain kind of cultural exchange developed against this background: one Sunday we would give a concert in the women's camp; the next Sunday they would perform in ours.

It is difficult to believe that this bucolic competition started up two months after the landing of the Allied forces in Normandy, at a time when Paris had been liberated and the eastern front was advancing toward us by leaps and bounds. The signs presaging the near end of the Third Reich multiplied, but camp life went on as usual. The commander of the women's camp made a special request of us: to have our double bass player give lessons twice a week to one of his female charges. He had just succeeded in "organizing" an excellent double bass, which no one could play. This would considerably strengthen the sound of his orchestra. After long negotiations, the task was undertaken by Heinz Lewin, who now had a little less work with watches.

The women musicians lived in a separate barracks equipped with a small stage on which vocal, solo, or chamber performances took place. They officially received a double portion of soup and supplements to their bread. Except for strictly musical activities, they were not burdened with any other work.

The conductor of the orchestra had been the eminent violinist Alma Rosé, who was known especially in central Europe. She was the daughter of Alfred Rosé, founder and first violinist of the world-famous Rosé Quartet. I was told that she had been a good friend and that more than once had stood up to the authorities in defense of the health or lives of her comrades. She had snatched more than one of them from the jaws of death, but in the end she herself took ill with typhus, which put a brutal end to her brief life.

On one of the partitions of the women's musical barracks

hung Alma Rosé's conductor's baton, decorated with a knot of black crepe.

◆　　　　◆　　　　◆

I am writing memoirs, not a study; I relate, make comments, but do not issue judgments. The main theme of my memoirs is music, but it is naturally connected with the background against which it was played, hence my entirely nonmusical digressions. One such digression concerns my experiences— bright and bitter—with non-Jewish Poles and the relations I had with some of them.

My first encounter with Poles, my countrymen, was not good, I would even say very bad. The circumstances were not conducive to friendship, to be sure. We lived in a world in which the German genius had invented, proclaimed, and put into practice an updated version of Darwin's theory. The species generally called human had been divided into roughly four categories:

1. Supermen, or Aryan Germans who loved the Führer and were obedient to his slogans and commands;
2. Men, or Aryan Germans who thought and acted differently than the Führer ordered;
3. Submen, or all other Aryans; and finally
4. Vermin, or Jews, Gypsies, and other dregs of the two-legged community.

This division comes as no surprise; the surprise would be that it was accepted as gospel by the *prisoners themselves.* And so the first category regarded the other three as "something worse," the second so regarded the two below, and the third so regarded the fourth. And the Jews regarded themselves as something worse than the Gypsies—as the worst of all. There was probably no Jew in the camp who dared to think that he was a man as good as any other. That would have been pure heresy.

On the other hand, separate from this hierarchy and segregation practiced by everybody, there prevailed in the camp another, tacit ethic whose distinguishing mark was the date of arrival in Birkenau, indicated by the number tattooed on the left forearm and repeated on the band of the left jacket pocket: a low number meant a longer stay in the camp, survival of the first mental and physical shocks, fortitude, and aptitude for organizing; all of this gave rise to a certain respect not only from the "better" categories of *Häftlinge* but also from the esmen. The prisoners with "fresh" numbers were contemptuously called "millionaires." I had been such a millionaire in July 1942, when I had the number 49,543. After two years, when the numeration had reached the 200,000s, I had long since been a camp VIP, Jewish to be sure, but I was "respected" more than many an Aryan millionaire, and not only because I was *Kapellmeister*.

When I landed in Birkenau, these customs were unknown to me. I had come there encumbered with prejudices inculcated into me by a world in which the word *man* meant something. Instinctively, I tried to join a group of Poles I had encountered— to speak with them, to share the thoughts oppressing me. Hearing the Polish language, I gathered up my courage, saying to myself: Good, countrymen from Poland, things won't be so depressing, we long for the same thing, they will tell me about Poland, I will tell them about France, arm in arm, and other naive things like that . . .

I was rejected as though I had leprosy. I was stupefied. I did not understand this instinctive, wolfish hostility toward a stranger. When for the first time, already a member of the orchestra, I went with the detachment outside the camp for *Arbeit*, which was supposed to make me *frei*, my supervisor, a Pole, a prisoner and musician like me, did not cease to drive and admonish us: "Work, kikes, work. Even so, you won't come out of here alive!" These were supposed to be words of encouragement.

Somewhat later another typical but also amusing incident took place. I was sitting on the lower pallet and dressing in haste. From the upper pallet someone called out, "Hey, Felek, hand me that shoe laying there!" Thoughtlessly, or rather inconsiderately, I shouted out, though this command had not been addressed to me, "You say hand me that shoe lying there, not laying there." My brother musician, but not in race, got down from the pallet, gave me two slaps, and screamed, "You, you lousy Jew, are you trying to teach a Pole to speak Polish?"

Against this firmament of hatred and contempt three heaven-sent stars of the first magnitude appeared in the person of three Poles, stars that will shine for me until my dying day. I write "three," but this does not mean there were not more of them. There certainly were. But fate had it that I did not meet others.

About one, Ludwik Żuk-Skarszewski, I have already written, certainly not enough, but we lived together for a relatively short time. Let me perpetuate here the memory of two lifelong friendships, which blossomed in soil that not only was hostile to their springing up but that simply nipped in the bud the possibility of close relations of this kind. Perhaps that is why during my two and a half years in the concentration camp I met only three Poles who offered me their confidence, affection, and friendship.

Ludwik Żuk-Skarszewski, Tadeusz Jawor, and Jan Stojakowski were the first Poles in Birkenau who spoke to me as one equal to another, as one man to another, Pole to Pole, Jew to Jew. After my and others' previous experiences, after having sunk to the bottom of the camp hierarchy, established and accepted by everyone—myself included—thanks to them I felt like a human being again, in a narrow circle to be sure, but this narrow circle seemed to me, and was indeed, large.

◆   ◆   ◆

Jawor and I found each other after the war—like Żuk and I did—thanks to a coincidence, or rather thanks to a tangle of coincidences. Jawor now lives in Sędzisław (Jelenia Góra Province) and subscribes to the Warsaw illustrated weekly *Świat*. In 1962 I published in *Świat* my recollections of the painter Tadeusz Makowski, whom I knew well.* The article was signed with my first and last name. Jawor did not believe that it was I, but he wrote to the editors and asked for my address.

These recollections had not originally been intended for *Świat*. I had written them at the request of Władysława Jaworska, a historian of art, who had written a monograph on Makowski. Since the publication of the monograph, a rather long one, had been delayed, and since November 1962 was the thirtieth anniversary of the painter's death, Jaworska sent my recollections to the editors of *Świat* with the suggestion that they be used to commemorate the anniversary. Jaworska's book was eventually published in 1964. If it had been published in 1962, there would have been no recollections in *Świat*, Jawor would not have read them, and we would never have found each other.

I learned about Jawor's experiences only after I entered into

---

* These recollections are reprinted in *Episodes . . . Epigrams . . . Epistles . . .* (in Polish) (London: Poets' and Painters' Press, 1976), pp. 147–51.

correspondence with him. In the camp there was a lot of time for the struggle for survival but not for imparting secrets. Perhaps it is worth quoting a few fragments of his letters.

I was arrested along with other colleagues (from railway repair shops) on 18 April 1941. We were charged with the distribution of the brochure "Poland Lives," published and circulated in Warsaw. . . . My Auschwitz number: 16,998. For the first few months I worked in the gravel pits near the gate of Auschwitz I, later on flood control of the Soła River. . . . When I was already completely worn out, swollen and lame, an acquaintance of mine from Stary Sącz, who had arrived in Auschwitz with the first transport in 1940 and had gotten a job in the bread warehouse, interceded on my behalf to have me accepted into the orchestra as a trombonist. He was on good terms with the director, Franz Nierychło, who was also the kapo of the kitchen. Nierychło agreed under the condition that they send me my instrument from home (for when free I had played in the railway band and had my own trombone). Through the authorities I wrote home, and the trombone was sent to me.

When the camp in Birkenau was established, part of the orchestra was transferred there. And so I met you in that camp, where we worked together until evacuation, i.e., till 28 October 1944. We met again briefly in Oranienburg, where I had come, along with my trombone.

In Birkenau I was bedridden for seven months with rheumatic inflammation of the joints. I escaped death in the crematorium thanks to acquaintances who worked as male nurses in the hospital barracks. When a visit by the Gestapo or the camp doctor was scheduled, they carried me out on a stretcher to the "healthy barracks" and carried me back after the visit was over, giving me a new "health card." Miraculously I managed to overcome (very slowly) this illness. My legs were weak for a long time. You probably remember that I used to go out for the playing of the marches much earlier than the rest of the group, since I couldn't keep up with the march pace.

Did I remember! I also remembered a lot of other things. Jawor also was quite a talented painter, and the condition of his legs excluded even the easiest work outside the camp. During a period when Danisch was less hostile toward the orchestra, Jawor somehow managed to get his permission to stay behind in the barracks to paint and generally decorate the vestibule and music room. I remember our long evening chats, sometimes amusing, more often melancholy, which served to tighten our friendship. How many times did I think to myself, why are there not more people like him?

When we were evacuated to Oranienburg, we traveled in different cars. After arrival and a brief meeting, our paths separated for . . . eighteen years.

✦   ✦   ✦

My third star is Jan Stojakowski. Number 577, one of the first Auschwitz Poles. He joined the already-mentioned Józef Waśko and Czesław Kluczny in taking English lessons from me. After some time the first two dropped out, but Stojakowski continued to the end. He was the supervisor of the food warehouse, so my income, rather than suffering, increased considerably. Janek presented me with bread, margarine, marmalade, sausage, and priceless potatoes, and thanks to him I also got an additional pot of soup from the kitchen for the orchestra. He shared news from the front that he had heard somewhere on the radio. (At the time I thought there was a secret underground receiver, but it later turned out that this news came from *Häftlinge* who worked in the esmen's rooms, where they often heard military and political communiqués.) From him I also learned about the assault on Hitler's life on 20 July 1944.

Jan Stojakowski was arrested on 2 November 1939 for "social and political activity." He was taken from the jail in Tarnów to Auschwitz I and in April 1942 was transferred with a group of fifty-two other prisoners to Birkenau. In the course of time he joined a small group of Poles that helped to organize escapes and whose members more than once gave it a try themselves. There were not many escapes, for the risk and difficulties were great. Not until July 1944 did Stojakowski have an opportunity to try his luck, but the attempt failed and had to be postponed until October. Janek describes these interesting incidents in one of his letters:

Kurt Reinhold was the *Oberkapo* of the *Zimmerei* (carpenters') detachment. His favorites were Józef Papuga (no. 12,049) and Kazimierz Andrysik (no. 89), and for this reason they had considerable freedom of movement and went where they pleased with their carpenter's work. Papuga took advantage of this and with a few trusted colleagues began to "organize" a barracks [hideout] for escapes in the region of B.III, which everyone called "Mexico." In this section there was an uninhabited barracks. Along one of the outside walls of this barracks was a high pile of earth from the digging of a drainage canal. Boards were cut out of the inside wall and a space was hollowed out in the mound that could accommodate a few persons. It was standard procedure in the camp that after the escape of a prisoner, the SS garrison kept watch for three days and nights on the large ring of watchtowers.* This time had to be waited out in the previously prepared barracks.

A former officer of the Polish army, Jan Dmochowski, an activist in the underground and also a political prisoner, became privy to this matter. He forced Papuga into agreeing that he, Dmochowski, would pick the first prisoners for the escape. His choice fell on the two Dzięgielewski brothers, Henryk (no.

---

* The camp was surrounded by two rings of watchtowers (*Postenkette*), one large and one small.

121,412) and Tadeusz (no. 121,413). Insufficiently prepared, they did not hold out the three days in the hideout but came out before the night watch on the large ring had been called off. The esmen noticed them. They caught the older one (Tadeusz), but the younger one managed to escape. This happened on 4 July 1944.

The next would-be escape was scheduled for 7 July. Those who took part were Kazimierz Andrysik, Józef Papuga, Stefan Szermiejowski, Jerzy Kapujczyk, Stefan Prałowski, and I. When Prałowski went into the empty barracks with a bottle of vinegar and pepper (as protection against dogs), he observed that he was being followed by some unknown prisoners. So he did not go into the bunker, but quickly informed Papuga. In this situation, it was decided to call off the escape. This happened on the day I said farewell to you—only briefly, as it was to turn out.

My successful escape did not take place until 18 October, ten days before the first, partial evacuation of the camp. My comrades were Tadeusz Lach (no. 22,488) and Wladyslaw Piłat (no. 330). I then said farewell to you for the second and last time. Our escape this time did not lead through the bunker. We came to an agreement with the driver of a truck that carried barracks panels with doorways. We hid in this trunk, covered by boards and other timber; the driver started at once, and by the time the camp siren gave the alarm all three of us were already in the forest.

I remember that sunny July day when Janek told me about his plan of escape, which no one else outside the group knew about. He told me at that time that if both of us survived, I could try to write to him at some address (which I did not remember) in Nisko on the San.

With Janek's departure I was left to some extent "without means of life": once again I had to rely on the miserable camp food. This was unimportant, though, since ten days later the partial evacuation of Birkenau took place. I moved out with a considerable reserve of calories and health, which Stojakowski had generously bestowed upon me over long months. They enabled me to survive the last camp period, when I once again fell from the heights of prosperity to the depths of poverty and degradation. Music belonged to the remote past. I returned from captivity physically exhausted, morally stupefied, mentally crippled—but alive.

Not long after my return to Paris, I wrote a few words addressed to "Mr. Jan Stojakowski, Nisko on the San, Pologne." After wandering around for a long time, my letter reached the addressee.

This was more than thirty years ago . . .

My correspondence with him, like that with Żuk and Jawor, has lasted to this day.

✦   ✦   ✦

Until now the war had been an abstract concept for us; it did not concern us. To be sure, it was known that they were fighting in the west, that bloody battles were raging on the eastern front, that the Germans were retreating everywhere, that the front was approaching us inexorably. But this approach was somehow endless and to us seemed very, very far away in time and space.

And now suddenly with every day it became less distant, and the signs of its approach increased continually.

The German army urgently needed reinforcements, and our esmen were healthy men, good brawlers and drinkers. At the beginning there had been more than two thousand of them; in time this number shrank to two hundred. Latvians and Ukrainians were recruited into the SS, but because of the numerous desertions caused by the approaching inevitable catastrophe, they were replaced in the camp by already-aged members of the *Volksturm* (People's Militia) and retired policemen. These men obviously had neither the training nor the mentality of professional Gestapo and SS men, and whenever they had the opportunity, they openly admitted to us that they were so only by virtue of uniform.

The atmosphere in the camp became unrecognizable; the discipline and terror slackened considerably, not just in reality but officially as well. An unheard-of command was issued: it was forbidden to beat the prisoners! Physical punishment had to be justified by a special report.

At the same time, the general living conditions of the *Häftlinge* gradually improved. The authorities began to equip the barracks with running water and other sanitary fixtures, as though expecting a visit from the Red Cross or, who knows, perhaps even from the enemy himself. The esmen began to suck up to the Jews, justifying themselves and throwing the blame on their superiors. Those who at one time had supplied the prisoners with German uniforms to enable them to escape were now looking around everywhere for civilian clothes and even prisoner's stripes in order to mix in with the civilian population or the crowd of prisoners. Escapes were more numerous than before and also more often successful: there was not enough personnel to organize a successful chase. The chain of the Beskid Mountains, visible from the southern side of the camp, was swarming with partisans, whose numbers were continually increasing with escaped prisoners from Auschwitz and the neighboring camps. The authorities seemed helpless.

◆   ◆   ◆

Lagerführer Schwarzhuber had been absent for almost two weeks. Supposedly he had been summoned to Berlin by the highest authorities of the Gestapo, it was said even by Himmler himself. A feeling of anxiety swept over us. I recalled the words of *Rapportführer* Joachim Wolff: "Not even one *Häftling* should come out alive from any concentration camp. . . . There will be no one who can tell the world what has happened here in the last few years."

One early afternoon I was sitting quietly in the *Musikstube* writing music when we were told that the detachments were returning early today and that the orchestra had to form up as usual on the stage to play the traditional marches. Similar orders and counterorders had recently become quite common, and we were not surprised at this change in routine.

Except that the time was unusual, everything went normally. The detachments were marching in an even, healthy step. Since the new regulations had been put into effect, one no longer saw corpses carried by the living or limping prisoners among the returning detachments. We were finishing the last march and getting ready to return to the barracks when one of the esmen suddenly gave us a sign that we were to wait. At the same moment, the silhouette of Commander Schwarzhuber appeared in the gate.

We did not believe our eyes. Schwarzhuber had changed past all recognition. We were approached by a hollow-cheeked creature swaying on its legs that in no way reminded us of the martial figure of the SS *Haupsturmführer* we knew so well. He came up to our stage, reeling and tripping over nonexistent obstacles. He was clearly dead drunk. He clumsily wrenched the baton from my hand, pushed me aside, and with difficulty took up his position exactly in my place. With a derisive scowl on his face, bordering on disgust, he raised the baton and blurted out, *"Spielen Sie nun 'Heimat, deine Sterne."* Nearby stood a group of esmen, who were looking on the scene half-amused and half-outraged. The musicians played as usual and safely reached the end, paying no attention to the snail-like movements of my replacement.

But a new shock was in store. The commander, apparently confused by the sudden silence, turned to me with glazed eyes, still holding the baton raised in the air, and asked, "Can you play for me the 'Internationale'?" I did not know what to answer, and all of us were aghast. Was it fitting to burst out laughing at a "good joke"? To simply say *nein?* To remain silent?

The first one to recover his presence of mind was Weintraub. He stood at attention and "reported obediently." "*Herr Hauptsturmführer,* unfortunately we cannot play the 'Internationale' because we do not have the music." "And why don't you have the music yet?" Schwarzhuber insisted with the obstinacy typical of drunks. After which, not waiting for a reply, as though pacified, he added, "It doesn't matter, you'll soon have it," and, continually swaying on his legs, he made his way inside the camp instead of toward the gate. *

We breathed a sigh of relief, though anxiety still gnawed at us: why had the commander gone to the square, where the detachments were lining up for evening roll call? Was this an ordinary drunken intrusion? We had to hurry, though. We packed up our belongings and marched back to the barracks.

The roll call took place in total silence, but strictly according to protocol, under the watchful eye of the commander. *Mützen ab! Mützen auf!* Attention! At ease! counting, submission of the report, and all the rest. But we waited in vain for

* Russian troops had just crossed the Bug River, on the border between Poland and Russia (15 March 1944).—ED.

Danisch's usual *Blöcke abrücken* (dismissed to the barracks)! Instead, we learned that *Herr Lagerführer* had something very important to announce to us.

The commander's voice, though normally loud, could not reach the entire camp. So he stopped in front of each detachment to make the same speech. We were in a state of great excitement. What did the commander have to say to us?

Finally, he stood before the group from our barracks. He was still tottering on his legs and expressed himself with difficulty, although he knew well the text of his speech, which he had already made several times. We got the impression that his own words intoxicated him still more. He stuttered, repeated the same words or even entire sentences, as though he wanted to convince himself of something in which he did not believe.

"Häftlinge!" he began solemnly, "do not become disheartened! Do not give credence to the supposedly alarming rumors spread by irresponsible individuals that the Germans have lost the war. Do not be alarmed by the air raids or the sounds of cannons. You are too far away from the front to know what the true situation is. The brilliant strategy of our Führer is to lure the enemy deep into the territory of the Reich in order to make him overconfident, which must end in his destruction! If he continues to press on, we will use poison gas. *Häftlinge!* Do not lose hope! Observe camp discipline! Do not try to escape, for you will be caught and severely punished. On the other hand, those among you who behave properly will soon be released. Long live our Führer! Long live Germany!"

The warm applause that greeted our orator clearly showed that we "had not lost hope."

◆   ◆   ◆

Aleksander Kulisiewicz, whom I mentioned in the first pages of this book and to whom I owe finding Ludwik Żuk again, published a long article entitled "Music and Songs as a Factor in the Mental Self-Defense of Prisoners in Concentration Camps" in the Polish periodical *Przegląd Lekarski*, 1977, no. 1.

The very title itself astonished me. To be sure, Kulisiewicz based his arguments on experiences from the Sachsenhausen concentration camp. Perhaps it was different there—though that is very unlikely—than it was in Auschwitz. Kulisiewicz quotes two contradictory opinions in his article. On the one side:

When exhausted in KL [*Konzentrationslager*] Auschwitz by a full day's work the prisoners came staggering in marching columns and from afar heard the orchestra playing by the gate—this put them back on their feet. It gave them the courage and the additional strength to survive. And then with the melodies of various marches played in the German style under the wild cadence of "links und links," we could clearly hear how our colleague musicians spoke to us in masterly fashion on their instruments, each of them in his own musical native language. They sent improvised greetings in colorful sound, a special *crescendo con agitato* [ever louder and stormily]: "Don't give up, brothers! Not all of us will perish!" What marvelous eloquence of this musical internationale!

This was written by a man named Kazimierz Gwizdka. And here is the opinion of a Jan Tacina, as quoted by Kulisiewicz:

The camp songs of the Poles became a treasure house of patriotic as well as lyrical creativity of such tremendous emotional content that it is difficult to compare with any other songs in the entire history of our musical culture. In the depths of degradation this was a powerful shout of protest against the physical and mental Hitlerite bestialities; an expression of bitterness, hatred, and rebellion, and especially of the most sublime, ardent faith in the preservation of humanity.

For me this prose is simply awful. I leave aside the musical amateurishness of the authors (*crescendo con agitato* does not exist and means nothing; musical internationale!), but to say that the "emotional content is difficult to compare with any other songs in the entire history of our musical culture" borders on complete ignorance of our "treasure house of songs" and "musical culture." The level of the camp songs was so unsophisticated, not to say low, that to compare it with the level of our heritage of songs is an insult, even if unintentional, to the latter.

Let us now look at the other side of the coin. Kulisiewicz also quotes the recollections of Romana Duraczowa:

We are returning from work. The camp is nearer and nearer. The camp orchestra in Birkenau is playing lively marches, popular foxtrots. It's enough to make your belly ache. How we hate that music and those musicians! Those dolls sit there, all in navy blue dresses and white collars—in comfortable chairs. That music is supposed to perk us up, to mobilize us like the sound of a war trumpet that during a battle rouses even croaking horses.

And here is a quote from Victor Frankl's book *Psychologist in a Concentration Camp:* "Music as well as all other artistic endeavors were too grotesque in the concentration camp; they gave the impression of art only through the ghastly contrast with the background, which consisted of desperate existence."

What conclusion can we reach from this? How was it really? Were or were not music and songs factors in "the mental self-defense of prisoners"?

It is difficult to make a judgment in the name of the millions of people who passed through the Hitlerite camps, whether they died there or came out with their lives. In the end, the supporters of one theory or the other were either witnesses of a small segment of camp life over a relatively short period of time or they base their opinions on documents left behind by the victims. One must also consider that the music played in the camps did not have the same effect on everyone.

I personally believe that music was simply one of the parts of camp life and that it stupefied the newcomer in the same way as did everything else he encountered in his first days in the camp and to which he gradually became "habituated" in time—up to the moment of complete acclimatization and callousness. Music kept up the "spirit" (or rather the body) of only . . . the musicians, who did not have to go out to hard labor and could eat a little better.

In the same issue of *Przegląd Lekarski* I read another pearl written by a professional musician, Adam Kopyciński, orchestra director in Auschwitz I:

Thanks to its power and suggestiveness, music strengthened in the camp listeners what was most important—their true nature. Perhaps that is why many certainly tried instinctively to make a certain cult of this most beautiful of the arts, which precisely there in camp conditions could be, and certainly was, medicine for the sick soul of the prisoners.

It is hard for me to believe that this bombastic claptrap came from the mouth of a professional musician who was a prisoner in a real Hitlerite concentration camp and saw there more or less the same things I saw in Birkenau. "Strengthened their true nature"! "Medicine for the sick soul"! In reality, the true nature of the prisoner manifested itself, with very few exceptions, under the influence of hunger, floggings, and illnesses; and the medicine for his "sick soul" was food and real medicines, not music!

Such a bombastic and pompous look at the role of music in the camps unnecessarily complicates a matter that is extremely simple if it is approached from the side of camp reality. To start with, one must be aware that in every camp there were two separate categories of prisoners: the VIPs, who were well supplied, and the paupers, who were condemned to perpetual starvation, hard labor, illness, and death.

The former did not need any "strengthening" of their "true nature." They had—except for freedom—everything their souls could want, and for them music was entertainment and an additional luxury for which they paid generously. One must also take into consideration that the music played in the camp cannot possibly be included among the "most beautiful of the arts" and that it was absolutely unsuited for any kind of "cult" by the listeners. This was instead light music for the masses; there was nothing in it that could stimulate any transport of the more noble sort in the listener. As regards the few more sophisticated musical pieces in our repertoire, they were listened to almost exclusively by the German prisoners and esmen.

For the class of paupers, however, if music had any effect at all, it had a disheartening one and deepened still further their chronic state of physical and mental prostration. To be sure, during Sunday concerts we were surrounded by a more or less numerous group of spectators of various ranks, and our music seemed to give pleasure to some of them. But this was passive pleasure, without participation, without reaction. There were also some who cursed, swore, or looked askance at us as intruders who were not sharing their fate. In any case, I never *even once* met a prisoner whom music perked up and encouraged to survive. The motto of the starving was: eat, eat, eat . . .

So much for "abstract" music. There remain songs and

camp tunes, which involve the living word, which is more capable of stimulating man to faith and deeds. But even here the matter is not so simple.

In addition to what I saw and heard myself, I have gathered information from friends and acquaintances all over the world, former prisoners of various concentration camps. Nearly all of them maintain that the songs that originated in the camps were vulgar, in local dialects, or even trashy and had nothing in common with raising people's fortitude, and that the songs and tunes that could be regarded as manifestations of the resistance movement were written *after the war*.

It is painful to shatter a myth. But it is even more painful to read that "precisely in camp conditions" music was medicine for the sick soul of the prisoners. For this is not true!

◆　　　◆　　　◆

As I mentioned earlier, Albert Haemmerle had left us, not long after his broken love affair. He had probably been sent to the front. In the camp there were fewer and fewer German *Häftlinge* of young or even middle age. All capable of bearing arms had gone to the defense of the threatened *Vaterland*.

In place of the ruthless Albert we were given another barracks chief, an older German named Joseph Hoffmann. He was a good-natured, weak-minded, always smiling Bavarian, and absolutely harmless. He shared with us all the news he heard and commented on the worst almost with enthusiasm, regarding these items as portents of Germany's certain victory. Apparently the commander's allusion to the crossing of the Bug as a "brilliant strategy" of the Führer's had made a big impression on him.

Hoffmann kept muttering about some new sensational

German weapon that would soon crush the enemies of the Führer. He also told us that all of the prisoners would be exchanged for German prisoners of war in the ratio of two for one. Another day we found out that two cars filled with handcuffs had been attached to the last train with Jews that had come to Birkenau. They were obviously intended for us. Several of us would be linked together. Soon the evacuation of the camp would start, obviously on foot, and the possibility of escape had to be prevented.

It was impossible to find one's bearings in this avalanche of contradictory pieces of information. We did not know what to believe. We lived in an atmosphere of feverish anxiety about our fate, about the fate of all the residents of Birkenau. And now at the moment when the evacuation of the camp was on everybody's lips, a new blow fell on us:

After long days of peace, which suggested that the inflow of crematoria meat had stopped, a string of trains unloaded on the Auschwitz platform new crowds of victims to be thrown into the flames. Where had they come from? It seemed that all of occupied Europe had long since been completely de-Jewed, with the exception of a few survivors who had succeeded in finding safe hideouts. It turned out that these crowds had been transferred from camps closer to the theater of war operations than ours.

This time, however, these really were the last arrivals, and I was the first one who, indirectly, was informed of this. They ordered us to spruce up and form ranks *zu fünfe* with our instruments for the march outside the camp. We were accompanied by six armed esmen. We were going to one of the crematoria. But probably not to the gas, which would harm the instruments. We were going to entertain those who gassed others.

The members of the *Sonderkommando* had worked without respite; they had performed tremendous services for the Third Reich and deserved a reward, like a last cigarette for a condemned man. The *Sonderkommando* had done its job; the *Sonderkommando* could depart. And could there be any more pleasant departure than to the sounds of music? Not for a German. So the authorities came up with the idea of arranging a special concert for the special detachment.

A few rows of benches for the musicians were set up inside the crematorium camp. There were no music stands, so we would have to play from memory, but we had come in a small group. At a sign from the esmen, we settled down and prepared our instruments. We were playing for people who would soon be incinerated, but by whom was a mystery. Perhaps by us? After all, the authorities had already involved the musicians in so many nonmusical jobs . . .

The concert lasted nearly two hours. We played among other things a few Jewish melodies, the same ones *Unterscharführer* Bischop had been wild about. In the pauses between one number and the next, we took advantage of the inattention of our guards to exchange a few words with the victims. Some of them lashed into us with curses, oaths, profanities.

After the performance was over, the members of the *Sonderkommando* gave us presents. "Take this, it might come in handy . . ."

A few days later we learned with shock that a rebellion had broken out in the crematoria area. Through the grapevine we heard that the crews of all four crematoria were scheduled to be liquidated by the esmen. A total of six hundred persons! They decided not to submit. For some unexplained reason there was a mix-up among the four crews and only two of them, the first and the third, went into action. The prisoners blew up crematorium III, cut the barbed wires, and escaped. The alarmed pack of esmen shot the two remaining crews to the last man and then organized a chase. All of the escapees were caught and killed.

This happened on 7 October 1944, three weeks before evacuation, eleven days before Jan Stojakowski's escape. Who knows whether this rebellion did not contribute to his success?

◆　　　　◆　　　　◆

A strange, ominous silence prevailed in the camp. Barracks chief Hoffmann was our only contact with the outside world. A veritable hail of news and retractions fell on us, none of it credible. Except for playing the morning and evening marches, the musicians had almost nothing to do, and everyone killed time in his own way. We stopped worrying about Hoffmann's news, according to which the camp was supposed to be evacuated tomorrow, the day after, in a week, in two weeks, or instead that it was supposed to be destroyed along with the prisoners and leveled to the ground so that the Russians would have no idea of what had gone on here. To top it off, the orchestra was supposed to move out with its instruments, so they had to be cleaned and kept in readiness. It was maddening.

We had no vodka, so we sought forgetfulness in music. Most suitable for this purpose was the string quartet, since the entire orchestra was too loud to be able to concentrate and forget. After inheriting the violoncello from the Czechs, and owing to the lack of a suitable repertoire, I had composed, or rather re-created from memory, my own four-part piece for this group, which we rehearsed when conditions permitted. One day I took out the movements from the pile of music written in my hand, and we sat down before the music stands. We played in a strange concentration, entirely different from the mood to which one had submitted in remote times of carefree freedom. Absorbed with rendering the most exact interpretation possible, we got through the first two movements without mishap.

Then suddenly a completely unknown esman entered the room. Apparently a new one, for he was no longer young. We jumped up like one man. I cried *Achtung!* We stood at attention. *Weiter machen,* the unwanted guest said mildly. We sat down and played the third movement, then the fourth, to the end. The esman asked,

"What was that? Whose music is it?"

I was surprised, for I had not expected such a question. After all, I could not say that I was the composer. In panic I quickly raced through my memory and suddenly got the idea of mentioning an Austrian musician who is not very well known, even in Germany. I stood at attention and replied,

"This is a string quartet by a composer called Karl Ditters von Dittersdorf."

"A very beautiful quartet. One could tell right away that it was German music."

And he went out. Ugh!

Through the windows we could see Hoffmann running back and forth as though he were looking for something. He was probably the harbinger of more news. Eventually something in this mass of information would have to turn out to be true.

Hoffmann burst in, bathed in sweat, and in a triumphant voice announced the most recent sensational news,

"And what did I tell you? Half of the camp is going to be shipped out. The orchestra, too, but without instruments. I know this from the *Blockführer* himself!"

If this were true, it portended nothing good. "Without instruments" meant that we would sink back into the depths of poverty. Hoffmann's words were soon confirmed. Part of the camp would be evacuated. Which part? Where? No one knew.

They put us through delousing and took away our clothes and underwear. In exchange we got new ones—rags. We looked like complete paupers. With misty eyes I looked at our beautiful *Musikstube*, said farewell to the instruments arranged in perfect order, to the pile of filled-in music paper, to the table at which I had sat safely for so many days, weeks, months. It is shameful to admit it, but I left Birkenau with regret.

Surrounded by esmen armed with submachine guns, along with the crowd of other prisoners, we headed toward the Auschwitz railway station, the same one that had greeted me two and a half years ago. Along the way we encountered a small group of officers, among whom I recognized our *Lagerführer* Schwarzhuber. He also recognized us when, passing him, we took off our caps in farewell. He turned to the rest of the officers and, pointing to us, gave a sigh in which one could sense pride mixed with pain: *"Meine schöne Kapelle!"*

Coda

◆   ◆   ◆

Here I could end the story about "Auschwitz melodies," for there was no more music. I should, however, supplement it with a few personal as well as historical details (for the two are intermingled).

The same cattle cars as before transported us to Oranienburg-Sachsenhausen, where we stayed for a short time. Leon Weintraub died there, and there I also parted company with Tadeusz Jawor and nearly all my previous companions.* We were scattered among various camps situated more to the west. I found myself in the group sent to Dachau, or rather to one of the many neighboring subcamps, called Kauferings. Mine was number 11.

We arrived in November. The winter was early and severe. We were cooped up in underground barracks, only the attic and roof protruded above ground. Every day at dawn we would go on foot from our Kaufering to the place of assembly, about two kilometers away. All of the other Kauferings gathered there at the same time.

Our work was to complete the construction of an underground factory, for what I did not know, perhaps airplanes or

---

* Not until after liberation did I find out that Heinz Lewin had been taken to Mauthausen, where he died.

maybe arms and ammunition. This was a closely guarded secret, all the easier to guard because we had no access to the
underground part of the factory: like our barracks, it rose high
above the ground in the shape of an elongated half egg or rather
like the back of a whale rising up out of the sea half a kilometer
long. A real monster.

Narrow-gauge railway cars loaded with heavy bars, beams,
bricks, stones, gears, tools, sand, and lime raced back and forth
along the back of this armored whale. In order to load the cars
the materials had to be taken from below to the very top of the
whale. The prisoners did this either singly or in pairs, though
having a partner hardly made the task any easier. Carrying the
material on an even level would have required considerable effort, but here one had to climb up a steep, slippery side without
any support for the hands or feet. In frost, rain, blizzards, for six
endless months. I could satisfy myself with calling these last
six months of my captivity "terrible," but it was something different, something I will not try to describe—and so much the
better.

On 28 April 1945 the authorities of all the Kauferings ordered a general *Antreten* or asssembly. This was three days after
the meeting of the Allied and Soviet forces on the Elbe and Bal-
tic and two days before Hitler's suicide.

In accordance with the accepted tradition, the commander—I do not remember his name—made an official
speech that was simultaneously a sermon and an admonition:

"*Häftlinge!* Today we have to leave this camp, even though
the factory in whose construction you took such an active and
productive part is still not completed. You will be exchanged
for German prisoners who are in captivity with our enemies.
Remember that you were treated humanely, in accordance with
universally recognized rules, and that you are to say this wher-

ever your destiny takes you. Thank you and I wish you a successful journey."

There was some truth in this speech: in the Kaufering we had not been beaten, and the food, though inadequate, had been much better than in Birkenau. This may be because we were watched by military guards who had never been esmen, and, in any case, it was the beginning of the end.

We moved out in close order, together with a group of guards. We walked for three days. We slept under the open sky, now in some forest by the road, now under a heavy rain without any cover. And on the fourth day at dawn . . .

. . . we woke up—FREE! There was no trace of the guards. We looked around the area, and it turned out that we were close to the small camp of Buchberg. We made ourselves at home there as we pleased, making excursions into the town for food and waiting for events.

On 3 May—another historic date—the Americans came. The first one I saw handed me a pack of cigarettes and said simply: "Hitler's dead. How're you? OK?"

✦   ✦   ✦

On 18 May I was already in Paris. After a few days of unending formalities (I had to prove to the French authorities that I was I) and reception festivities prepared in honor of the returning survivors, I got the urge to go to the movies. I do not remember the film, but one scene from the newsreel fixed itself forever in my memory. On the screen I saw a series of deafening explosions and then a swirl of iron, fire, and smoke rising in the air, along with a shower of flying and falling fragments, blocks, and pieces, like the explosion of a furious volcano. The commentary said, "On . . . the American army blew up the German underground arms factory in Kaufering not far from the Dachau concentration camp."

This was "my" factory! "My" whale! My last stage! I felt a little strange. So much work for nothing.

Paris, January–June 1978

Appendix

Three Warsaw Polonaises

I

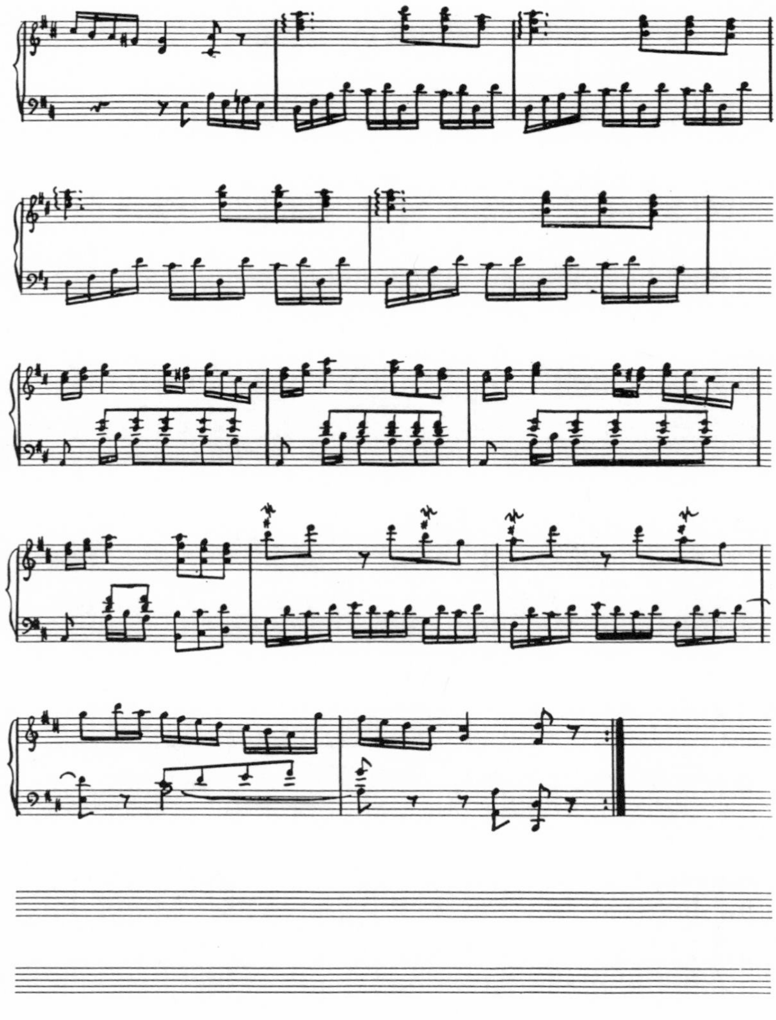

II

Andantino con espressione

III

Allegro energico

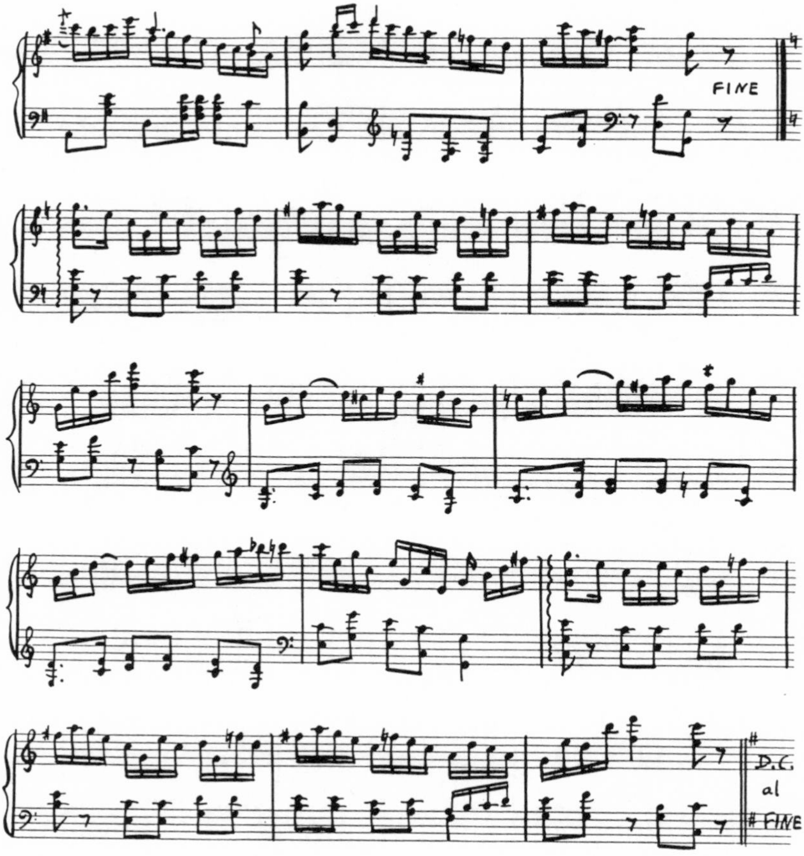
FINE
D.C. al FINE